THIS PETTY PACE

THIS PETTY PACE

Robert C. Tibbs

Copyright © 2005 by Robert C. Tibbs.

Library of Congress Number: 2004195135
ISBN :   Hardcover   1-4134-8000-4
                Softcover   1-4134-7999-5

All rights reserved. No part of this book may be reproduced or transmitted in any form or by any means, electronic or mechanical, including photocopying, recording, or by any information storage and retrieval system, without permission in writing from the copyright owner.

This book was printed in the United States of America.

To order additional copies of this book, contact:
Xlibris Corporation
1-888-795-4274
www.Xlibris.com
Orders@Xlibris.com

26142

CONTENTS

History 15

Foreword 29

This Petty Pace: The Father's Tale 31

One With Nineveh: The Uncle's Tale 58

The Forest Of The Night: The Town Crier's Tale 106

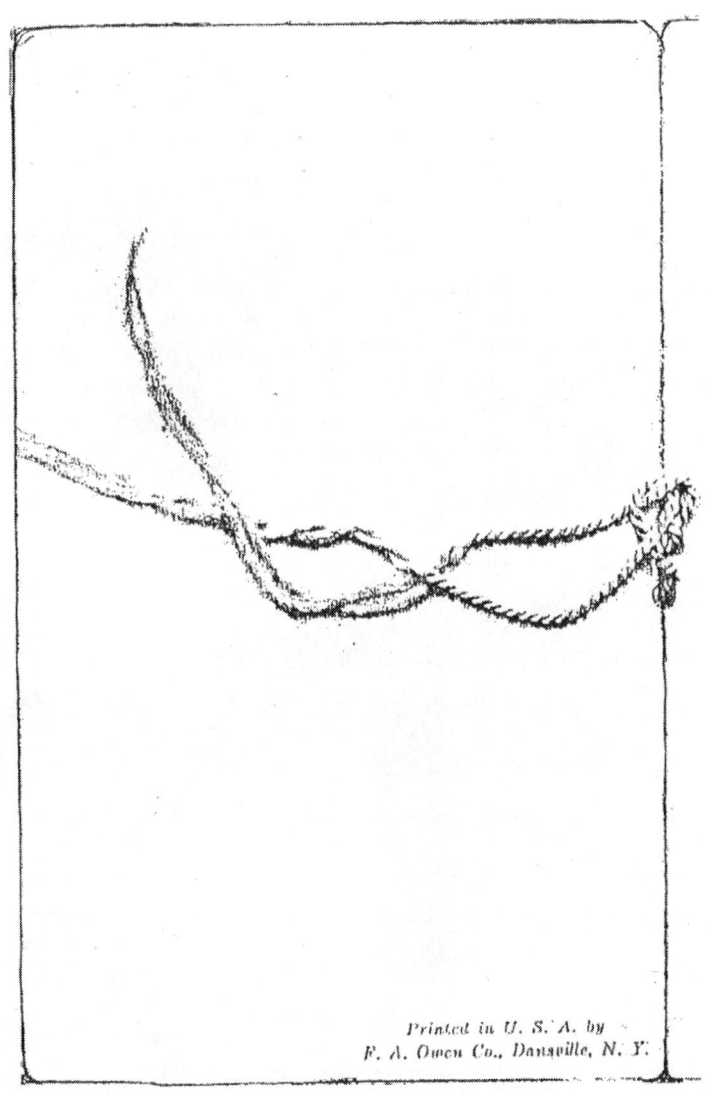

Printed in U. S. A. by
F. A. Owen Co., Dansville, N. Y.

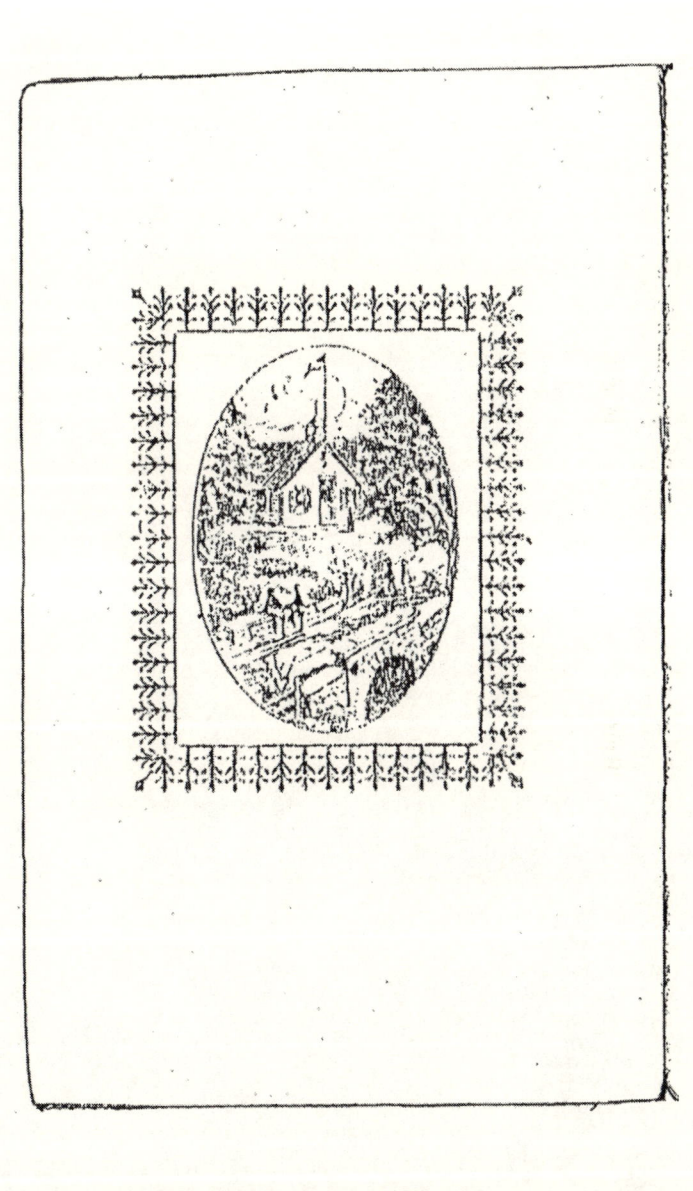

History of Hushpuckena School

1885-1930

For

Pat, who has put up with me for forty three years and our four sons, Bob, Ashley, Bentley and Clint.

History

In compiling the History of Hushpuckena School we found past records had been destroyed, hence our facts have been obtained from the storehouses of memory. We are indebted to Mrs. R. C. Tibbs, Mrs. R. R. Murphree, and Mrs. C. B. Taylor for many incidents herein recorded. These facts are authentic, yet there may be incidents of real worth omitted which might be of interest to many former patrons.

Such facts as we have been able to obtain we are sharing with our friends and postgraduates who will ever cherish a tender memory of "Hushpuckena School."

Hushpuckena School was opened in September, 1895, and has been in session continuously thirty-five years.

The first term was held in a church which formerly stood near the little cemetery south of the town. The record of this term we have been unable to obtain.

The second enrollment was six:—Clara Tibbs, Maud Tibbs, Herman Downer, Carrie Mason Jeffries, Brookie Jeffries, and May Boatwright.

This little school was taught in the homes of the people; two terms in the home of Mrs. R. C. Tibbs.

Next a little cabin on the outskirts of the town was used, until in 1899 Mr. D. J. Allen gave the lot upon which our building now stands, to be used for school purposes.

Messrs. Tibbs, Jeffries, Daugherty, and Feather erected a small one-room building, the nucleus of our present comfortable school house.

Later on, this building was repaired, home-made desks installed, each child furnishing his own desk. The seats were home-made benches without backs. A turnip patch near the school furnished a relish to noon lunches.

On through the years the little school struggled, sometimes gloomy, discouraging days—sometimes cheery, sunshiny days, when teacher and pupils were optimistic.

Then came the dark days when war-clouds hovered over. The little school furnished several representatives, two of whom were Oliver Jeffries and Lamar Love.

As the clouds lifted, the little school pressed onward. Again a bit of repairing; a few bought desks, a globe and a teacher's table were installed.

The older pupils had now passed out, some to College, some to the business world, some to home-making.

Soon with the growth in population and wealth the little village felt the need of better school facilities, hence, gave their attention to the improvement of the school and surroundings.

To Mrs. Ina Griffin of Clarksdale, Miss. (nee Miss Ina Wilkinson, Shelby, Miss.) belongs the honor of first grading the school thus laying the foundation of a promising outlook.

The County Superintendents have been especially helpful in the progress of the school. The first Mr. Tom Owens of Cleveland, Miss.; second Mr. Armstrong in 1914; then our present much respected Mr. A. K. Eckles. To him the school owes much of its success.

In 1920, under the regime of the present teacher, the first graduate from the Elementary School passed into High School—Mr. Roland S. Murphree, now of Itta Bena, Miss.

Dr. Wyatt, of Shelby, gave the first graduating address, and awarded the first diploma within the walls of Hushpuckena Schoolroom. The "Parable of the Talents" was his theme.

Since then nineteen graduates have passed on, and such speakers as Dr. O'Neal of Chicago, Rev. Madison Flowers, Shelby, Rev. Moss, Rev. R. G. Lord, of Duncan, Rev. McCorkle of Shelby, have obligingly lent their oratory to grace our Commencement occasions.

In 1924 the school grew so rapidly that a primary room

and an assistant became necessary, the enrollment at that time being seventy-three. Mrs. W. B. Pemble (nee Pauline Herrington of Merigold) was the first Assistant. She was followed by Miss Louise Field, Centerville, Miss., Miss Ida Lena Hearn, Memphis, Tenn., Miss Sara Lee Miller, Memphis, Tenn.

Music was now added to the curriculum. A new piano was bought, and all necessary equipment installed, including a library, and a phonograph.

A three hundred dollar playground equipment was put on the campus, including the latest improvements.

A Tennis Court, a basketball team, a baseball team did their part in the athletics.

A Parent-Teachers Association helped in the upbuilding of the school.

Besides the Commencement Exercises many beautiful entertainments have been given, all pointing to the uplift of the community. The happy Christmas time has ever been a joy to the children and their elders, so much so that when Duncan laid her covetous eyes upon us and consolidated, a postgraduate exclaimed, "No more Christmas trees!"

When the present teacher entered the school in September, 1919, Katharine Rogers, then five years of age, was the baby of the school. She will finish in Shelby High in 1931, never having failed in a grade. She was chosen to represent her class on Field Day, 1930, an honor won by highest average.

May 23, 1930, her brother, Vince Rogers, has the honor of being the last graduate of Hushpuckena Public School. His father, Joseph Rogers, has been a trustee and staunch supporter of the school.

That the school has made good and has done its part in the upbuilding of the town and state we have but to mention Mr. Robert Tibbs, Mr. Eugene Tibbs, of Hushpuckena, Mr. Roland Murphree, Itta Bena, Miss.; Mr. J. W. Johnson, Leland, Miss.; Mrs. R. R. Murphree; Mrs. C. B. Taylor; Mr. and Mrs. J. A. Feather; Mrs. B. E. Masters; Mrs. Morgan Kimbrough; Mrs. Brookie Holt; Mr. T. B. Moore; Mr. James Shelton; Mrs. E. D.

Harris; Mrs. Charles Gibson, Mrs. Lester Summers and scores of others who are accomplishing much in High Schools of the state, or filling honorable positions elsewhere.

May 23, 1930, we came to the closing of Hushpuckena School. With the trend of the times it had to lose its identity, being absorbed into the life of Duncan School. Yet memory will keep alive the hours spent in the dear class rooms, the lessons learned, the friendships made which will be renewed in Eternity. Eternity alone will reveal the harvest.

Hushpuckena School will ever be a treasured memory to those who have had the privilege of working within her walls.

County Superintendents

Tom Owens   Mr. Armstrong
            A. K. Eckles

County Health Officer
Dr. R. D. Dedroylder

County Health Nurse
Mrs. Charles Clark

Trustees

R. C. Tibbs   Mr. Jeffries
Mr. Daugherty   A. D. Murphree
Con Day   G. W. Williams
I. L. Moore   Joseph Rogers
George Summers   R. R. Murphree
J. A. Feather   J. C. Reed
Shannon Joseph   C. B. Taylor

Teachers

Miss Julia Chandler	1896-1897
Miss Tillie Montgomery	1897-1899
Miss Sidney Williams	1899-1901
Miss Willie Neblett	1901-1902
Miss Kate Love	1902-1903
Miss Ola Dubois	1903-1904
Miss Evelyn McCoy	1904-1906
Miss Berniece Johnson	1906-1907
Miss Lizzie McBain	1907-1908
Miss Susie Cox	1908-1909
Miss Clara Tibbs	1909-1911
Miss Maud Tibbs	1911-1912
Miss Clara Tibbs	1912-1913
Miss Ina Wilkinson	1913-1914
Miss Nina Crawford	1914-1915
Miss Rose	1915-1916
Miss Nancy Sullivan	1916-1917
Miss Alma Murphy	1917-1918
Miss Alma Jeffries	1918-1919
Miss Jennie D. Howard	1919-1930

Graduates

1920

Roland S. Murphree — Itta Bena, Miss.

1922

J. W. Johnson — Leland, Miss.

1924

T. B. Moore — Skene, Miss.
Avis Jones (Mrs. Gee) — Ackerman, Miss.
Winnie McElveen (Mrs. Wilson) — Baton Rouge, La.
Della Val Feather (Mrs. L. Summers) — Florence, Miss.

1925

Josephine Rogers — Hushpuckena, Miss.
Geneva Shelton (Mrs. Sorrell) — Itta Bena, Miss.
Lovie Ann Sheffield (Mrs. L. Brooks) — Cleveland, Miss.

1926

Gladys Sheffield (Mrs. B. Livingston) — Ruleville, Miss.
Lillian Bounds — Crowder, Miss.

1927

John Brooks — Deceased
Robert Brooks — Hushpuckena, Miss.
Katharine Rogers — Hushpuckena, Miss.
Richard Murphree — Hushpuckena, Miss.
Falba Cotton — Clarksdale, Miss.

1928

Kathleen Sharp — Hushpuckena, Miss.

1929

Susie Murphree   Hushpuckena, Miss.
Martha Reed   Paulette, Miss.

1930

Vince Rogers   Hushpuckena, Miss.

Pupils

Leila Mae Allison	Dorothy Alston
Elizabeth Atkinson	Willie Bayliss
Sallie Bayliss	Mae Boatwright
Aline Boatwright	Robert Boatwright
Cora Bono	Joseph Bono
Nancy Jane Bono	Lillian Bounds
Ruth Bounds	E. L. Bounds
Vivian Bounds	Janie Broom
Elmer Broom	Pat Broom
John Brooks	Robert Brooks
Mabel Brooks	William Brooks
Z. A. Brooks	Marvin Carraway
Rena Carraway	Winnie Carraway
Russell Carraway	A. P. Carraway
Myrtle Cotton	Iva Cotton
Falba Cotton	Mary Willie Cotton
Oleta Cotton	Paul Cotton
Joe Crawford	George Crawford
Russell Day	R. P. Day
Hansel Day	Hugh Day
Arthur Dalehite	Herman Downer
Wilbur Dalton	Raymond Dalton
A. M. Dalton	Matilda Edwards
Eva Edwards	Edith Embree
Roy Embree	Beatrice Embree
Z. T. Faulkner	Lena Feather
Robert Feather	Amos Feather
Aldine Feather	Della Val Feather
Robert Feather	Florence Feather
Bobbie Fiebelman	Lizzie Floyd
Thelma Fletcher	Leora Fletcher
Talah Griffin	Effle Griffin
Ike Griffin	William Griffin

Thomas Griffin — Lucy Griffin
Buford Hall — Velma Hall
Gladys Hall — Pauline Havard
Paul Hernandez — Amelia Hernandez
Hilton Hunt — Elizabeth Hunt
Genevieve Jeffries — Oliver Jeffries
Joseph Jeffries — Hubert Jeffries
Carrie Mason Jeffries — Brookie Jeffries
Avis Jones — Ettie Jones
Melvin Jones — Doris Jones
J. Hugh Jenkins — J. Linn Jenkins
Pauline Jenkins — J. W. Johnson
Mary Johnson — Percy Joseph
Jennie Joseph — Bert Joseph
Bert Joseph, Jr. — Audrey Mae Joseph
Clifford Jordan — Jessie Jordan
Russell Jordan — James Jordan
Kellum Jordan — Maudie Lee Jordan
Melvin Joyner — Earl Joyner
Jessie Joyner — Gladys Joyner
J. D. Keeton — Luther Keeton
Estelle Keeton — Ozie Mae Keeton
Neal Leftwich — Imogene Leftwich
Heber Leftwich — Julia B. Lockhart
Hutchinson Lockhart — Maggie Love
Sallie Love — Albert Love
James Love — Charles Love
Lamar Love — Tarleton Mattingly
Lelia Martin — Brown Martin
Helen Moore — J. H. Moore
Garnet Moore — Ethel Moore
Katharine Moore — Omar Moore
Ada Moore — T. B. Moore
Weldon Moore — Roland Murphree
Sarah Murphree — Lucille Murphree
Julia Murphree — Richard Murphree

Susie Murphree	Winnie McElveen
William McGann	J. B. McKnight
Shelby McPeak	Dock McPeak
Edward Morgan	Allie Mae Nason
Lucille Nason	Jennie Ruth Norwood
Gholson Oswald	Maud Oswald
Mary Parker	Ethel Parker
Berry Parker	Fred Parker
Curtis Parker	Percy Parker
Walter Pruett	Camilla Pee
Roy Pee Mary	Pauline Pridmore
Mike Pyle	Francis Pyle
Claudine Pyle	Martha Reed
John Reed	Adolphus Reed
Jessie Reed	Malcolm Reed
Josephine Rogers	Katharine Rogers
Vince Rogers	Johnnie Rogers
Wilbert Rowland	J. L. Sartin
Geneva Sartin	Kermit Sanford
Anne Scarborough	Millard Smith
Louise Smith	Sydney Shepherd
Mattie Shepherd	Rosie Shepherd
Lovie Ann Sheffield	Christine Sheffield
Gladys Sheffield	Alva Sheffield
Isabel Sheffield	Gilbert Sheffield
Eldridge Shumaker	Ollie Shumaker
Kathleen Sharp	Mabel Sharp
Albert Sharp	Ruby Shelton
Geneva Shelton	James Shelton
Ruth Stevens	Estelle Stevens
Robert Stevens	Camille Summers
Eva Steen	Clarence Steen
Howard Steen	Clara Steen
Doy Steen	Lavelle Steen
Juanita Steen	Christine Taylor
Clara Tibbs	Maud Tibbs

Mae Tibbs	Robert Tibbs
Eugene Tibbs	Delilah Topper
Dempsey Topper	Angelo Topper
Florence Topper	Olcie Whittaker
Edward Whittaker	Glenn Williams
Martha Bell Whittaker	Weir Williams
Wiley Wood	Perla Mae Woods
Annie Bell Woods	J. T. Woods
Melvin Wells	Leslie Whittle
Pauline Whittle	Louise Whittle
Alonzo White	Walter Whiteside
William Whiteside	Louis Whiteside
Martha Whiteside	Hazel Winter
Wallace Wilburn	Hugh Wilburn
Mabel Winborne	Joe Winborne

Louis Westbrook, Jr.

Program

May 23, 1930

March	
Invocation	
Salutatory	Imogene Leftwich
Our School	Song
"A Mortifying Mistake"	Pauline Havard
Violin Solo	Kathleen Sharp
"Our Beloved School"	Florence Feather
"Hushpuckena School"	Christine Taylor
"An Appreciation—Mothers"	Johnnie Rogers
"Vacation"	Lucy Francis Griffin
"Last Day of School"	Heber Leftwich
"Our Bonnie Grad"	Robert Feather
Piano Solo	Christine Taylor
"Pirates"	Neal Leftwich, Bert Joseph
"Spare Those Books"	Vince Rogers
Testimony to Graduate	Audrey Mae Joseph
Letter, Gifts to School	Vince Rogers
School History	Mrs. R. R. Murphree
Retrospection	Josephine Rogers
Valedictory	Vince Rogers
Address	Supt. A. K. Eckles
Awarding Diploma	Supt. A. K. Eckles
Song	

Foreword

This Delta of ours has been different and difficult since it was created. It was not formed at the mouth of a river or stream as a delta should have been, but sideswiped by a mighty river that wiggled and turned as it wandered over the land, then flooded yearly for untold centuries covering it with a fifty foot layer of thick alluvium. When seen by the first settlers, it was a boundless, illimitable forest, dappled by swamps and briars and evergreen cane breaks, only traversed by Indian paths, stagnant streams and the predators and their quarry that lived here.

Seven thousand one hundred square miles of this thick alluvium comprise our Delta. Bigger than four states and almost as big as several others, the dark brown, friable land is some of the most productive in the world. For agriculture it is some of the youngest land in this country. Though parts of it along the river and a few other isolated inroads were cleared and farmed during the late antebellum period, most of the land was cleared after the railroad came, in the 1880s. I can remember my Daddy talking of land being deadened and cleared after he was a grown man and seeing the late afternoon sun cloaked in a pall of thick, blue-gray haze from piles of burning trees.

The earliest settlers here, in the antebellum era, were sons of some of the aristocratic Virginia or Kentucky or Carolina planters. They came here with their slaves and cleared relatively small acreages for the purpose of growing cotton and getting rich. A few farms still bear names from that era. All of this was on some of the higher ground along the major rivers, but the bulk of the land and all of the more flood-prone and swampy parts were cleared after the railroads came. The people who did this were tradesmen and small farmers, moving here from a wide area. It is these hard working, ordinary people, certainly absent any pretense toward aristocracy, except the nobility of hard work and dedication to family, who gave us this land and it is to these people we are indebted.

These stories are about some of them. They are from memory of experiences I had and tales I heard while growing up in a tiny Delta hamlet, then often visiting there years later. Most are from my father and an uncle, who liked to spin a good yarn and I spun the yarn further and commented on it even more. The lay-out of the town and Sugar Hill are accurate, as are some of the episodes. The account of the revival in the Chinaman store is based on my attending three revivals there as a young teenager and are ninety percent fiction and commentary, though the preacher's text is as authentic, as it could be from memory. There are a few word groupings and a rare phrase, taken from memory, of something read in the past. The preacher's quotes from Genesis, of course, are readily recognized.

THIS PETTY PACE

The Father's Tale

Tomorrow, and tomorrow, and tomorrow
Creeps in this petty pace from day to day
To the last syllable of recorded time,

Shakespeare
Macbeth

I was drawn over to Sugar Hill again today. The gravel road creeps through Hushpuckena, past the old deserted store and gin, then curves over the abandoned railroad just south of the trestle. The same trestle that had seen two hangings and Charlie Bradley's engine, 1066, crossing over it a thousand times at seventy miles an hour. It then turned and twisted as it slid down across a new bridge over the creek, then another sharp corner to the west and a straight half mile across the bottom to the hill.

Sugar Hill, a low flat ridge, was born in another time, out of the dissolved, transported earth from half a continent away. It had once formed the western bank of the river that brought it here, but was now a long level bluff suddenly thrown up out of the bottom, where the river itself had once run, swerving and boiling in its restless trek to the gulf. Like an orphaned child, the bluff was born here, then later abandoned, as was the rest of this delta, by the ancient roving river, fifteen miles away.

The gravel road across the bottom had been raised since it was put here in 1923, keeping it above the winter and spring flood waters, sure to come as the seasons. Still, trees and bushes lined each side, almost tunneling it as they had done since the first bear and deer eons before had marked its path, lined and covered it then by dark, hulking cypress and gum and water oak, now only by the second growth delta hardwood, spared by the tenant's ax, no longer here to need its warmth in a winter cabin.

On to the west the low ridge lay. There like a brooding giant, spread across the sky line forever stretched from horizon to distant horizon, the road carving a gaping opening across its face straight up its side. At the crest of the hill I followed the gravel north and wound around toward Maudie's old house and stopped in front of the ancient, sagging store, a bygone relic and once center of delta plantation living and stability. It was unseasonably warm for mid January, temperature in the 60s, with no breeze at all, the sun bright as July. Sitting there in the shade close by the front of the vine-covered time worn building, not a human in sight, not even a dog barking, only an occasional bird call in the distance, it seemed that time went back almost 60 years and I could see it was it was then.

The store was white and well kept, not a board out of place, the front porch solid with shiny worn, whittled benches on each side of the entrance and along its outer edge. Inside the shelves were filled with all the necessities, everything from baking powder to sugar, matches, canned sardines and salmon, snuff and tobacco, salt meat, fat back, and skins, sacks of flour and meal, coffee and tea, pepper, nutmeg, cinnamon and cloves, clothes like overalls and denim jumpers, cotton sacks, mule collars and leather harness, everything a farmer needed that he didn't produce himself, even coal oil lamps. In a back room there was an office with ledgers on a high desk that had a matching tall stool, a hand cranked telephone on the wall next to the door, a fireplace and hearth on the opposite wall. Desks and stools must have been high then to keep the bookkeeper's feet above a cold floor. I remember the smell of that store. It was like Daddy's store in Hushpuckena. The warm smell of corn meal, of nutmeg and cloves, of new leather and oiled pigskins, all this together and varying a bit, just a bit as you moved from place to place in the store. A side room ran the entire length of the north side of the building and about 20 feet further to the north, under the shade of a pecan tree, there was a lighthouse. A small 16 x 16 foot building which housed a "Delco plant," batteries and a small electric generator powered by a one cylinder water-cooled gasoline engine. This produced the electricity for the lights and several ceiling fans in the house and store. On further still opening toward the east, there was a "gear room," a storeroom for mule harness. Each mule had his own harness-gear-there, trace chains, back band, collar pads and collar, hames and bridle, plow lines all hanging from a row of racks along the wall, the mule's name painted in bright letters just above it.

If you didn't know them, each mule looked pretty much alike, long eared, big and dark brown, except the occasional gray one and rarely a red mule would be in the lot. But they were different. Each with his own temperament and stride. Some sulky, sullen and stubborn as a post. Others could be ridden quite well with a saddle. The tenants who plowed them knew each one by name and always demanded his own mule.

Since before Egypt and Mesopotamia, for more than 15,000 years muscle power had produced man's crops and still 50 years ago this was being done. The same wheel turning along a seemingly endless path. In the delta the mule and his partner provided most of that muscle. The mule has been called a pariah and many other worse names but he was rather a matchless, noble creature and he was one of the prime resources of this delta. If it had not been for him and his partner, both captives, save for a few river settlements, this delta would never have been settled. Together they cleared the land, grew the crops and restrained the roving river. He was a rather strange creature, long ears, head too big, a rough coat, short bushy tail, everything about him out of place. He resembled neither parent, had no children, and though more beautiful to a delta cotton farmer than a thoroughbred, he was abandoned by his embarrassed mother as a young colt. He has survived a hard winter on sticks and snowballs to pull a plow all spring and summer, then harvesting a cotton crop for an apostate, rogue farmer. He will work for you until he drops dead where he stands and he'll survive a climate where only man and mosquitoes can endure. I have seen him stand alone all day, facing a frigid wind, in the corner of a small barn lot, like a well-wrapped Tibetan lama at a high mountain shrine, meditating on eternity. He is now no more, his time has passed, but the sun will rise and the sun will set, the seasons will churn and the years will roll, this delta will never again see his likes, for at one time he and his partner strode with mighty, though muffled steps, across the cotton-covered plains of this alluvial land.

Just beyond a narrow road that ran outside the gear room a big barn loomed high above a broad, board fence, topped by a huge hayloft that held enough hay to feed the mules for months. Across the way there was a five hundred gallon water tank on iron legs forty feet in the air and a blacksmith shop. A blacksmith was there on the place, as important to the farm then as mechanics are now. Further toward the south a manager's house stood in a small shady grove, with fig trees on two sides of it. South of the store, connected by a concrete walkway, stood Maudie's big, white house. The length of the walk was columned by a row of tall slender Lombardy poplars, trees that had been brought to this country from Europe, probably two hundred years before. These majestic, statuesque trees, no more than three or four feet in diameter at their greatest width, had branches that came out from a central trunk, then rapidly turned and ascended straight upward, lying close together, forming a tight leafy shaft, reaching sixty feet into the air. Close by were low, spreading, deep green juniper bushes, hedges, and pecan trees which shown as a sharp contrast to the yellow stemmed, palm sized leaves, buff green and pale, covering the Lombardies. The trees rose up in a distinct margin, almost a wall along the walk. The firm, waxen rigidity of the plastic like leaves offered a broad surface to the slightest breeze, producing a constant rattle high up in the branches, when hardly even a stir could be felt on the ground. Often rowed, these obelisk forms were set on lawns and in parks, along roadsides and driveways all over the delta. There were some in our yard and most yards had them. The trees frequently were grown to outline or frame a building or garden. The tall columns sketching an edge or border around any area where they were placed. Many school yards were surrounded by them and their rows frequently offered shade to farm headquarters but the towering, lanky trees, brought here from a cooler Europe, were not hardened to the warm, humid, insect burdened, flat lands of this delta and they lasted here only a few years, at their tall magnificent best, slowly succumbing to insects and disease.

 Then for a short time, where these once proud sentinels stood, only their decaying remnants lingered. Holding yet to a little more time, like an unseen portent, of the illusory era, that was the brief delta cotton economy, about to pass into oblivion.

Maudie's hip roofed house had wide screen porches running the entire length of two sides and part of another one. Screen porches were as essential to houses then as were chimneys and several hours each day, during warmer weather, were spent on a porch front or back, whichever was shaded. The porches on Maudie's house were exceptional. A big adequate back porch but the front porch extended across the entire south side of the house and also around part of the east. A wide swing hung from the ceiling on one end surrounded by porch furniture of several sorts, seating 8 or 10 people on a summer evening. Sonny and I spent the night there often and a favorite activity was running and racing on that porch. Maudie had a set of "Uncle Remus Stories" and that always was an enticement to an early afternoon nap and early to bed at night. We slept in Christine's bedroom and I remember now the ivory furniture and there was a fireplace. She had a player piano with 30 or more rolls and this was always a delight. A wind up Victrola, a big piece of furniture about 4 feet tall was in the living room. I remember a record, "Beautiful Red Wing," probably had been there 20 years when we found it. It must have been a catchy tune for we played it numerous times. Listening to a record, while sitting there in the living room on a thick, heavily stuffed, dark, blue couch, the only light coming through a single floor-length porch window, then gazing up suddenly toward a shadow-covered open doorway, you could often see a form dart quickly back into the gray murky darkness of another room. We had Thanksgiving or Christmas dinner there several times, the whole family, 20 or 30 people.
    There was a stir of activity on Sugar Hill during the growing season, for most of the place was planted to cotton, turn road to tree line and all was cultivated by muscles, the mule's and his partner's, but also a big garden and strawberry patch just to the west of the house to be kept hoed, chickens and turkeys to be kept up and fed. About an acre or so of grass to be mowed regularly. A rose garden and shrubs weeded, a tennis court spread out south of the house with a pecan

orchard to the west. The best growing thing there though was just off to the east of the house. A two acre peach, apple and pear orchard. There were peaches and pears that ripened in early June, just when Sonny and I were hoeing a one acre cotton crop we had just at the top of the hill, a road's width from the orchard. About 9 o'clock we would have to drift into the orchard and that usually ended the hoeing until the next day. Early peaches and soft pears bigger than oranges. At 9 o'clock they were still cool from the night before and the evaporating dew which partially remained. After an hour or so there we had to go see Maudie and finished with a chocolate milk that she made with added cubes of ice in an aluminum hand shaker. I don't remember ever drinking chocolate milk that approached it.

There was a "smokehouse" where hams and shoulders and bacon were smoked and hanging in rows on high racks, preserved year round. A cellar kept home-canned vegetables and fruit and preserves in a narrow temperature range year round and even longer, sometimes years before they were eaten.

The top of the store was adorned with the crown jewel of the place, the very insignia of authority, a 100 pound silver bell, that called all to work and to rest, and the bell's high, clear, singing, melodious voice was obeyed like a king's summons, sounding at sun up, at high noon, and again at 1 o'clock, its toll was a clarion cry, understood by all. Only a lap baby and the infirm were free of its beckon. It rang with a sharp, clear, penetrating tone that pierced the air like an arrow towards its mark and came across the bottom bearing on Hushpuckena so we heard it there full and distinct as if only a short distance away. There were others to the east of us, out at the Burroughs' place and another one to the south, on Allendale, where Mr. MacCurley managed, each with its own distinct, characteristic pitch and intensity. The bell on Sugar Hill, though, was preeminent with a clarity all its own. Its call had a crystalline quality and resonance that would linger in the air and surround you, then sink into you again and fade only slowly as it spread in the distance and passed away into echoes. The other two bells would emit a tone of lower pitch, with a sluggish dullness of shorter duration, that would pass by and rapidly wane and dwindle away, like a wooden maul against buried pewter. It would have been easy to know which bell had tolled, even though you were not aware of its direction, like a coon hunter knows the call of each individual hound, off in the woods on a misty moonless night.

Gibby Howard, "The Hostler," who lived close by, a jolly, grinning faced fellow, had the job each day of ringing the bell. He was an older man when I knew him, but he would rise from a sick bed to ring that bell. He couldn't miss a day, afraid someone would have his job. Gibby had done it for years and he had developed somewhat of a ritual, almost a ceremony or system of rites for his bell ringing. Around 11:30 or so he would leave the cotton field and walk to the store, sitting under a shade tree close by, quiet and meditative, noting his watch, a Waterbury, until a few minutes before noon. He would then rapidly march to the bell rope, tied high on a post by a water barrel at the side of the store. There he would stand, immobile and erect, like a pagan priest invoking the gods, or a white-robed preacher standing in mystic solemnity at the water's edge of Hushpuckena creek, just before entering for a baptizing—probably a similar stance was taken by King Canute, standing on the shore of the North Ocean commanding the ebb of the tides—his watch in his left hand held high above his eyes. The other hand was stretched out overhead grasping the rope.

As the hour struck he would loudly announce, "dinnertime," and bring life to the bell. With Gibby's hand on that bell, the tone was sharp and sure, almost burning in its intensity and cutting as a fine-honed edge. All the dogs in the area felt this and set up a course of howls. I heard others ring it and I had done it many times, but nobody could bring from it the voice that Gibby's hand would extract. Once standing close by as he rolled it, I heard him issue a low mournful tune, in rhythm to the dog sounds, like an ancient incantation, his eyes, glazed, set deep and dark in his round, solemn face, fixed to the distant horizon.

Gibby wanted all to know, the one man on Sugar Hill, who could pronounce the sun's position and prescribe the time. His call at noon was in rapid sequence and the fields would clear before it ended, but at 1 o'clock the strokes were slow and measured, solemn, like church bells tolling the death of a bishop. He had been told that people in Duncan and Shelby set their clocks by the ring of his bell and his act was performed with grave seriousness and almost pious resolve.

I once saw some tractor drivers and field hands sitting on the store front, in Hushpuckena, at noon and they got still and quiet and listened as the bell rang. R. B. Berry, one of the tractor drivers, a boy of 22 or 23, sitting there, raised up and loudly proclaimed in a slow, preemptive voice, "Mr. Howard can sho tome dat bell." He then walked out in the street and gazed straight up toward the sun, as if to check the accuracy of Mr. Howard's call. Standing there, he pronounced again, "Lawd, dat man sho can mark dat sun," sure that Gibby had correctly called the sun through its arc to its appointed zenith. With a quick tilt of his head, he added, "You know dem white folks in Duncans and Shelby sets dey clocks by Mr. Howard's bell." He then waved his hand and pointing an outstretched finger toward me, his head cocked to one side, he continued, "He gotta be right, dat man sho knows what he's doin'." He walked a short ways, then turned and kept talking in his loud, authoritative, confident voice, "When he tomes dat bell," and he pointed his finger again, "you better set yo clock." With an easy swagger he went on back in the store, confident and assured that all was right with the world, the universe is in good hands.

Daddy told me that it once had occupied a belfry on Jefferson Davis' plantation south of Vicksburg or Natchez, but the story of how it ever got to Hushpuckena had been lost to the pressures of time.

Gibby had lived in a three room tenant house less than a quarter mile away. The same house was later occupied by Cutter

Fog, who earlier had killed Lonnie for stealing his hay. When this happened, Cutter Fog lived out on the Falkner place and after this brazen premeditated murder he stayed locked up in his house, closeted there for 10 years until his case was finally dropped from the court docket. Sometime during the mid 1970s Cutter Fog moved to Gibby's old house which by then had electricity and shortly afterwards he owned a television set. He would come over to the store and in a low whispering voice tell his compatriots there what "that man on television" had said to him the night before and his hours long conversation with him, relating in great detail each one's comment and reply. One winter evening he was over in the store commenting to a small group about a recent conversation he had had with "that man on television." Bob was standing close by listening, but pretending to be busy at something else, while Mr. Cutter Fog eyed him with sideways glances as he unraveled another tale he thought to be true. About that time Harry, with the DTs, burst through the door hollering, "Ya'll better look out. There's a big bull comin' through that front window up there." They all stared in silent disbelief, Cutter Fog stopping his story, and after Harry had run on back in the office and was calmly seated before the fireplace, Cutter Fog whispered softly toward Bob, "Wonder what's done happened to us, I'il boss?" One hallucinator wondering about the faculties of another. Bob seemed to have been surrounded by a menagerie of clowns and buffoons, like being at a perpetual vaudeville or minstrel show, stories and comedies that probably helped him retain his sanity. Mr. Fog did, however, retain enough contact with reality to only whisper his visions.

Like most tenants then, Gibby had no electricity, no running water, no screens on his open windows to protect against the swarms of marauding, predatory, delta mosquitoes, but there was always that quick easy grin he gave everybody.

I had often wondered what could cause him to seem so happy. Maybe it was because he knew as long as the store shelves were full, he would never be hungry. Also, he had a house whose roof never leaked and it was surrounded by a forest of chinaberry trees which kept it the coolest house in the humid heat of the delta.

I well remember how much cooler it seemed in summer under a chinaberry tree and thought it must have been the huge mass of impenetrable tiny leaves emitting more water vapor than others. Most yards around had chinaberry trees then. The trees had a dense, close, compact canopy that formed a tight ceiling only eight or so feet above the ground. We had one in our front yard and Sonny and I shot marbles under it all summer. You never play marbles, marbles are always shot, another lost art, and we thought we were experts. Usually, one of our buddies from across the tracks, too young to hoe cotton or pretending to be sick until his family left for the field, would come over and shoot with us. Leland was always there.

Shooting marbles was one of the bright summer games of a long childhood that seems now to have burned bright like a meteor's flash, then gone forever, but others followed to take it over as we had done, though only for a short while. Marble shooting, by adults, was done in colonial America, probably brought here from England where it had come from the Middle East or China, but now it seems to be too slow, replaced by gadgets with computer chips and motorized, wheeled horses.

Though there were other trees and sunless areas in the yard, that shade under the chinaberry tree was always the coolest and usually even when the air was motionless and heavy under every other tree or shadow, a slow cool breeze would filter through it.

Surely, that was the secret Gibby's inscrutable grin was hiding. He had plenty to eat, an unfailing, permanent roof and a cool place to sleep during the hot working months of summer. Later, however, I came to suspect that it hid much more. It was, though, as natural and essential for him as breathing, always there and helping him just as much.

After awhile, a cloud drifted over the sun and a cool breeze whispered by. I got into the car and drove on past the house, to the south and turned west toward the pecan orchard. I got out and walked a ways through the orchard, gazed to the north toward the indian mound and the sand dunes. That was the first land that Papa—my grandfather—had farmed when he came here in a box car with horses in the 1880s. He said that he had stepped on every square foot of land in that 80 acres and had stepped on every square foot of it more than one time. To the west and south, wheat spread in a vast sea of emerald green, probably the first time that place had been in wheat since it was cleared of trees before the Civil War.

Standing there 60 years ago you could have counted 10 or so houses on that place, double that number within eyesight, where 100 to 250 people lived. Old people sitting on vine-shrouded porches, children playing in yards and barefoot along the dusty roads, people hoeing cotton and plowing mules in the spreading fields, some of the houses surrounded by paling fences and trees, chickens in the yard. All the houses in late afternoon with smoke drifting from the chimneys year round preparing an evening meal.

A woman may walk by leading a jersey milk cow on a chain or a red hog on a rope, maybe a boy leading a goat with haywire around his neck taking them home from a roadside grass patch where they had been grazing all day. Several tenants, riding the mules they had plowed since sunup taking them back to the barn for the night with a croker sack for a saddle, the pumice-like dust, to keep the two sweats from mixing, increasing the chafe, or maybe the sack was to keep the mule's sweat off of them. An entire community spending their lives from the time of their birth until they died there on Sugar Hill. Professor Hull may have walked by going to teach school in Hushpuckena at White Plains Church or going to a chicken dinner and all day singing there on Sunday.

I walked toward the road at the edge of the orchard and gazed down it toward the west. The fertile ground, moist and soft as it is in January, pressed down deep and firmly held each shoe imprint as I walked. Leaves covered most of it but they had lost their brittle crack and shuffle of fall and pushed down now against the moist earth, dark and close, as if they knew they would soon again become a part of it. The sunlight filtered down through the leafless barren braches that stretched out across the pale sky like thin silent pen scratches across a widespread blue canvas.

There at the sky line, just to the south, was a remnant of the old syndicate barn, its cypress timbers still standing, now used as an implement shed, and close by a metal shop taller than the barn had ever been. A huge white fuel tank lay horizontal a short distance away. The plagiarized name, "Sugar Hill Farms," emblazoned on its long side.

Further to the east on a slight rise was the site of a big log house and barn with outbuildings, the old Rembert place, probably built before the Civil War or shortly afterwards, now long demolished. Papa and Granny had lived there and rented the land. Bob was born there and during this time Granny's father had sent them $5,000.00 and told them to buy some land. Papa kept the check for about a year and sent it back, telling his father-in-law he "didn't want to lose his money on any of this delta swamp."

The fields were clear and sunny, the distant horizon or tree line seemed to be miles away. I remember a day like this when I was sitting in front of the store. Daddy was there and we were talking about something, probably the poor weather. The chinaman's store was operational then and a Chinese fellow, Joe Tong, ran it. He was also known as Jimmy Joe, two first names, nobody ever questioned it. He was Chinese, he could do that, supposed to be different.

"Jimmy the china-man" had a cousin, Thomas Mellenger Chew, much younger than he was, working there with him. Thomas was a jovial sort of fellow always ready with a grin. He and Bob used to box. He walked out on the store front that day while we were there and Daddy asked him what he thought about the weather. Thomas walked to the edge of the concrete and after scanning the sky and surroundings for a while turned back and said, "Prettier day I never see." That's just what I was surrounded by, one of the prettiest days I had ever seen, certainly for January.

After a while, though, a few high clouds raced across the sun, driven by winds I could not feel. A shadow passed over the orchard. Then, a silent breeze began to brush by. I felt it cold without a coat and a light haze seemed to gather and lay on the fields. It had formed so slowly I had hardly noticed and it only seemed to be in the distance and lay close on the wheat. After watching it a while, I could see there were some buildings out across the field within the haze and soon it was apparent these were tenant houses, the same buildings of 50 years ago. I even recognized some of them, those along the road that I had passed numerous times, particularly Pryor Davis' old house with the picket fence, the one Bill Scott later lived in.

The breeze pushed on and gathered to make a low whispering sound that moved in a slow wave across the tall wheat stalks. It moved with slightly more force on down the road and gathered more speed across the fields and seemed to dredge and push the haze and roll it up and heap it in a faint veil of mist or smoke above the road. It hung there like a low gray fog over a stream in winter.

It had been clear all afternoon, a bright blue sky, hardly a cloud in sight as the fog hovered there close over the road and settled down on it as the wind quieted to a breeze then hardly moved at all.

I turned in the opposite direction and behind me there was nothing above or on the horizon but the bright blue sky. Gazing back toward the mist settled over the road, I saw it had become more dense and within it there had begun a slight churn and a stir. It slowly widened and thinned as it spread out onto the field again over the wheat. It hovered there a while, quiet and motionless and seemed to press down into the wheat stems. I thought it would move on out over the wheat and dissipate and for a while it seemed that it would. It lay there thin and still for some time, though it completely hid the wheat as if gathering strength from it. Then it began to churn and stir again and with a more rapid movement it curled up together and crashed back over the road like two giant waves smashing together to moil and finally formed there a dense column of clouds.

It lay there like an opaque cloud module, narrow as the road extending to the west and upward to mix with the sky like a shaft extending down from it to the earth. Still there was the white sun, clear, almost cloudless blue sky, not a twig moved on any tree nor a sound from across the fields. After a while the twisting and churning began again within the compact mist and it started a low trundle along the road toward the orchard.

All the sunlight from the fields had gathered there within it to appear frosted white and toward its upper parts almost incandescent. It continued on along the road and when it was within five feet or so of where I was standing it stopped, but the slow moil and turn within it continued.

After a while the center portion of the cloud column began to clear and I could see deep within it. Then down the road a ways a silent, black-suited figure, carrying a small brightly painted box with strange markings on it, was slowly walking toward me. A human form as if it had been created out of the mist. There was a gold watch chain across his vest between his open coat lapels and above his smiling face a dark brown derby sat squarely on his round head.

When he was about even with me, still within the leading edge of the moving fog, he stopped. Not five feet away. I could see that same slow smile and as the white teeth shown within the dark face our eyes fleetingly met. A smile like that of an old friend. A knowing smile and with a hardly noticeable squint of an eye and a quick short motion of his chin, he seemed as if he had just solved a deep riddle. His expression was not that of a contemptuous or arrogant smirk, but a perceptive and understanding grin and surprisingly it made me feel relaxed and trusting. The fog stopped its moil and twist and he stood as real and certain as someone you would meet on the street and still the same easy grin with the deep crinkles at the corner of each eye.

In an instant I seemed to know, this must be Professor Hull, the schoolteacher who had taught school at White Plains Church. Professor Hull, long dead, when I first heard stories about him as a boy, not five feet away in the edge of a thick opened fog. The same knowing grin I had always heard he had and the deep set dark eyes above that grin seemed to hold a wisdom and a strength I wanted him to share and that I would never forget.

It seemed we did not need to say anything as we stood there and I was surprised that I seemed to feel some kind of bond or attraction between us.

His brown leather spats sharply contrasted with his spotless black shoes and black pants. His hair glistened in the sun. His white shirt beaming. A shine on his smooth ebony face like he had just walked out of a tonsorial parlor at the low end of town rather than down a wet January dirt road. In a moment he turned and looked back down the road from where he had come and slowly pointed in that direction.

Walking out into the road and standing next to him at the opening of the fog, I saw as if viewed from a high mountain peak a vast wide vista stretching for miles in every direction. There was a far-reaching prairie and to the far distant east a cloud-topped range of mountains extending endlessly toward the north and south with a wide snaking unspanned river curling along the edge as the prairie began. A wagon train was moving across it with mounted horsemen and cattle trailing along each side, then a sod house with several people milling around as if engaged in some type work, then a boy and a dimly lighted house with a blizzard howling outside and he walked up to the door, removed the key from the lock and a stream of snow, fine as dust blew back six feet through the room, out of the keyhole. The boy with his family had come to South Dakota around Sioux Falls from West Virginia. His father had been four years in the army of northern Virginia, but most of his cousins and even an uncle had been with the army of the Potomac. When the war was over the family was still badly split and his father had brought his family along with others of like siding, in a wagon train, to homestead on the black Dakota prairie.

A nineteenth century frontier town with mud streets and inside a store there, that same boy, who was fifteen years older was trying to sell an old man an oversized brick as a foot warmer. The old man gazed up at the boy, now a man, with hard piercing eyes, cold as stone and said to him, "Son, a young man like you ought to be doing something better than this." The young man had a wife by then, a young girl from Tremont, Illinois, who had been visiting Sioux Falls with her father there in the summer because of his asthma. Her father had a leather tannery back in Tremont and a factory that made saddles and boots and he had sold a great deal to the union army during the war. He must have saved a little money and was able to retire in his later years.

Then a railroad box car pulled by a steam locomotive for the past weeks from Sioux Falls, South Dakota, was parked on a side track and the same young man now older was leading two broad draft horses out of the car and he took them, while riding one, through a narrow tunnel of giant cypress trees, across the bottom to a long, flat hill of raised level ground a half mile away.

To the far side of the opening there was a twisting river and as I was drawn closer to it, I saw a stern-wheeler with billowing stacks slowly move to a landing. There were stores and other buildings facing the river and a town joined close by. There was a warped-board sign, hand marked and hanging on a leaning post with the words "Australia Landing" on it and I knew the long sand strip in the river must be Pushmatahaw Bar.

A freight wagon with eight oxen, the same transfer means used there for 150 years before the new railroad had come through, was leaving the landing. I saw it move through the woods, where four foot trees grew in old healed cotton rows, to a farm toward the same long, flat hill and the farm headquarters, where a big house stood, that I recognized as the Donaldson house. Some distance away I saw the young man putting his horses in a small barn lot made with rail fencing and close by a log house that was no more than two rooms with a dog trot through the center, the same construction used at Plymouth and before, found in Gaul and Britain by the Romans.

I turned back toward Professor Hull. There he stood, that same knowing grin like he had seen this all before, the dark brow-hooded eyes deep and glistening. He still didn't utter a word. His mouth never moved. He only raised his arm again and pointed through the opening toward the distant images.

There was Front Street in Memphis across from Confederate Park as it must have been at the turn of the century. Just above the river where only 50 years before a battle of ironclads had put Yankees in control of the bluff city, a market, which later became the National Garage, covering half a block with 20 butchers busy over carcasses of pork and beef and mutton.

Just down the street a big grocery store also opened onto Front Street facing the river. It was owned by a Mr. Clarence Sanders, a good friend of the black-haired German boy, Ed Fell, who owned the meat market. A short time later Clarence Sanders started Piggly Wiggly Food Stores, the first self-service food stores in the country and probably also the world. Sometime later he built the Pink Palace as a residence.

The black-haired German boy moved to a gray stone house on Sledge Avenue, then at the eastern edge of town, with a high board fence around the back yard enclosing the servants' quarters. The depression of the 1930s got Clarence Sanders, he never lived in the Pink Palace, and the depression or Mr. Ed Crump got the black-haired German boy. During the "Roaring 20s" he had made a great deal of money in his market that had been started by his father, but fast cars and numerous trips to St. Louis and Chicago took most of it and he must have saved but little, thinking good times would last forever. But, he did manage to stay in the gray stone house on Sledge for another 14 years. There it was, the house and street corner a short ways out in the fog and it brought back memories of visiting there when I was five or six years old.

Then that same young man still with the draft horses and added mules, now middle aged, living with his family in another log house, a bigger one, on the Rembert place. This changed quickly to a house made of boards on the west side of the bottom. The first board house he had lived in since he had left South Dakota. Then he was in town, in a store building next to another frame house and he stayed there a while but later to go on to a brick store and a bigger house where he died as an old white-haired man.

I saw my Daddy as a young man wearing a necktie, recently out of Mississippi State, plowing up in the north bottom, the fertile black earth turning in wide thick ribbons, mellow and crumbly, like water, from a fast moving boat's prow, with two mules pulling a turning plow.

Then he and Bob were sitting in front of the store as my mother walked up. Across the railroad to the north an old gray hand painted truck came knocking down the gravel road toward the store, the running board on the driver's side not four inches above the ground, the opposite side two feet. It came on up in front of the store and stopped next to the platform. Dave Thomas, a tenant farmer who married a widow owning a forty, got out, and after closing the door and tying it with hay wire, walked toward the store. Daddy spoke to him and said, "Dave, that was a pretty good rain we got here this morning. Did you get any up on your place?" "Yessuh, I sho did," he answered. Dave stood there awhile, gazing around, then looking up toward the sky in several directions, he continued, still standing in the middle of the road. "You know, Mr. Genes, that rain was worth something." Then, narrowing his eyes, furrowing his forehead, and with a fixed gaze he continued in a loud, ponderous, prophetic voice, like he was reading from the Bible in church, "Dat rain was worth twenty thousand dollars to Bolivar County." He stood there in the road not moving, a five gallon coal oil can in one hand, the white of both eyes easily showing from thirty feet, awaiting agreement with his estimate. "It was worth quite a bit," Daddy answered. "How are the crops up in your section?" he continued. "Well, they pretty good, Mr. Genes, but they's gettin' to be more tractors in the fields now and you know it takes mules to make cotton." They were there close by on the store front and the four of them turned and gazed directly at me. I started to walk toward them just as someone pulled my arm and I turned to see Professor Hull standing close by.

He stood there, the painted box with the strange markings still in his hand, the same easy grin, the deep eyes made even darker by the shining ebony of his face and glistened even brighter like two shining lights from a cavern at night. I tried to look back toward the fog, but he nudged my arm again. I asked him what he had in the box. He didn't speak, but only seemed to ponder my eyes, with a quizzical or puzzled expression on his face.

I knew it must be important to him. He had carried it held close, since I had first seen him. Maybe it was an answer to the riddle he had solved. The cause of that relaxed, easy grin and his knowing, unconcerned, quiet eyes. He must have known my thoughts, for when I said that his eyes changed, the smooth grin was gone. He put his hand on top of the box as if to open it. I moved closer. He held it up so as to let me see easier within it. His eyes became more intense, not furious or violent, there was no rage in them but more concerned, like maybe it would be better for me not to see. He hesitated a brief moment, then slowly gazed up at me and our eyes easily met again as the top and the box slowly began to separate.

As the inside of it broke into the light, I knew I would soon know its secret. I leaned over further and saw deep within it as it narrowed toward the bottom. The inside was as bright as the exterior with the same strange markings. Then I saw the bottom of the box. It was smooth and reflective and shown like its other surfaces. Painted and marked like the outside. There I saw the blinding incandescence of the high module, glinted off of it, like sunlight from a Heliographer's mirror. That was all, there was nothing else, only the reflected light. The box shown empty.

I gazed back at his face. The eyes as before had narrowed, the glisten still gone, they were darker and seemed even deeper than before. Still, they held that strained concern. His mouth formed as if he would speak. I waited. His chin moved slightly like he was trying to make words to explain it. I waited longer but no words came.

He then turned and pointed down the road to the east toward the hilltop away from the mist. I saw nothing there and I turned back toward the mist.

The road and fields were empty and bright as before. The cloud was gone. A warm mid afternoon sun hung in its place high above the tree line. I turned back to Professor Hull. He too was gone, like the mist that had formed him.

I stood there again with only the green fields, the empty winding road, the barren leafless trees. To the north the indian mound rose against the sky line. I heard a car, top the hill and saw it go on to the south. I wondered why Professor Hull hadn't told me. Maybe he must have thought that if I had not understood after all he had shown me, a few words would mean nothing. Maybe he showed me some of the people I owed a great debt. Certainly that was true and I could only pay the debt in the opposite direction to the east as he had pointed and to the future.

Maybe, too, he had said that the real having and knowing is the longing and yearning, the search for it, like chasing for an answer, the search for security and happiness, the search for faith and God, the search for knowing. Maybe it was something else.

After a while I walked slowly back into the orchard gazing again across the spreading fields where every dark, green blade stood alone and quiet in the cool winter sunlight. I thought about how this delta looked just a few short years ago, when I was younger.

There were fields of cotton, spreading fields, shoulder high, in precise plumbed rows, then white with the autumn, reaching from horizon to fading horizon. The Mississippi River to the west, the Sunflower and beyond eastward to the red hills, nothing but cotton. The fields just for a while, just for a short while, from early September were almost solid white, the pure whiteness of a welder's arc, like bleached sunlight, a clear, brilliant, starched whiteness that seemed to impart a special virtue all its own. A hue that gave the fiber a certain royal preeminence and imperial tone shown by no other, a glow to mimic even the radiance of a miser's vault. A place and life for itself, a place and life for some living here.

Cotton had an enticing allure, a certain seductive magic and attraction, the illusion of potential wealth and its permanence, but for many it was merely a siren's song.

Fields of cotton, empires of cotton, the total complete sustenance of this delta-cotton. Some here, recently successful, soon thought themselves to be aristocratic and secured a mail-order coat of arms and manufactured heraldry and genealogies, particularly if they lasted into the second generation, even before any member of the family or relative had passed freshman English. Nonetheless, as soon as possible one would be off to the university with pennants and flags to show.

When the few finally made it to Memphis, old man Ed Crump's fiefdom, then to join a country club, then later, from the mid 1920s until the depression, more to party at the Peabody, they knew they had finally arrived.

When a group would make one of those Memphis trips, they would announce it over the countryside and it would be the talk of the area for a week or two. A group from a nearby town had recently returned from a weekend at the Peabody and of course that was the conversation for the winter. Daddy was talking to old man Buck Burroughs in front of the store one morning and asked him what he thought about those traveling folks and their Memphis trips. Mr. Burroughs was slow to answer, but after he looked off in the distance for a while, as if thinking about it, he turned and looking straight ahead said slowly, "Ah-God-suh, they better stay close to shore. If these folks don't watch it they're gonna soon eat their seed corn." He hesitated a moment, then turned toward Daddy and continued with his eyes glaring. "And it's gonna be too late 'fore they know it." Mr. Burroughs was right about some, but they didn't know it.

"That was the good life, forever!" Some were sincere and assured of their permanence when they elected make believe royalty with crown and scepter, functionaries in cardboard and painted plumage, the sparkling regalia of a distorted vision, to preside over elaborate balls and outings for a night or a week. Others merely for a good romp, for the merriment and to frolic. Any excuse for a spiritus illusion to abate the thought of mortgage and taxes. Some even learned to drink blended scotch whiskey rather than Papa's whiskey, bourbon, had accounts at all the stores in Memphis, Neiman Marcus and New York, some even sent checks across the Atlantic to London and Paris. All on borrowed money.

With one good crop these happy people played and danced and imagined a good time, thinking all to follow would be similar, they made a fleeting stab at artificial opulence. Then suddenly, it seemed, a price collapse, extravagant and lavish spending or jarringly unfavorable weather would put them "back in the road" from prodigal to privation, in only a short span, but they had had their good time.

Their land may then be bought by a broken-speaking immigrant, brought here indentured, or a previous frugal tenant, supplied by a Memphis merchant.

The cycle would start again, resuscitating once more the old call and yearning to make a permanent and enduring show, to say, "I am here, I too am important."

The same voice, but with more skill and forethought, built the pyramids and Solomon's temple and Rome. The same voice, with more skill and forethought, built the buttress-supported, intricately carved, caverns of Medieval Europe, those sacred stony halls, fixed in time, vibrating with melodious chords, chanted in that ancient, Tiberian tongue, thrust high upward, a direction known only to gravity-bound man. Where for a thousand years, the altar stones have been caressed and worn by the same black-robed priest, already a millennium old, when the first stones were set.

Some here, however, were of a softer more perishable clay, most wiped out by the first wind, ground away by the shifting sands of ignorance and illusion even before the first stone was raised, not one drop in the ocean of time. Brought by the benighted and hopeless mentality, which seeks show and ornament, as a distraction from their intolerable loneliness and void, an opiate to mask the reality of emptiness and debt. Like insects suddenly flourishing in a warmed malarial swamp or blossoms on a transiently thawed, Siberian tundra.

They may have answered again, "But I had my day, the pharaoh had no more. Stone is for those who can see it, those who have use of it. The dead stone, neither will it fix a moment in time nor will it defeat it." Some would say, "But they were blind for they didn't grasp it, their eyes were shut, it was never the stone but its placement and the markings upon it."

All this now gone, vanished, a casualty of petroleum driven engines and synthetics, electronic images and sounds. The wheel was broken. A different future lay ahead.

The energy base changed, muscle power no longer its source, this whole world changed, like the change wrought by capturing the energy stored in black powder rather than that in the bent branch of a yew tree or that released by heated water replacing that gathered by widespread canvas.

The last of the Lombardies, once majestic and proud in their towering columned rows had crumbled and dissolved back into the earth thirty years before. The last tenant house disappeared ten years later. The tenant once upright and proud in his essential place had gone long before that, replaced by offices in New York and Chicago and Zurich with names like Monsanto, Deere and BASF, taking part of the crop even before it was planted and all of it before the first bale was at the gin.

The dwindling occasional plot of genetically altered cotton, now, painfully manicured and precisioned by twelve-row leviathans and artificial moons. The mule not seen for two generations and some of the descendants of his partner, those left behind, doled in rowed hovels around the edges of decaying towns, though some, like Professor Hull, teaching school and others, mayors and in the congress.

As I stood there in the winter stillness of the orchard, I saw the smooth green fields, soft and mellow as an old painting, extending on, wave after rolling wave, empty and lonely toward the horizon, a trackless dirt road, forlorn and deserted, winding into the distant tree line, a solitary hawk floating above the indian mound. There was nothing to say that any of this had ever happened. It could have been a dream or a fantasy or as legendary as Atlantis.

After a while, I turned and through the trees and overgrown bushes I saw the old paint-flecked white house, a porch wrapped around its south side, a chimney next to a window. There it was, all of it. Close, though another time away; hovered there in the trees and bushed in, it loomed silent and empty toward the crest of the hill. In memory, inviolate as the spirit that raised it and the dark healed earth upon which it sat. In time, ephemeral as a passing whisper and doomed as a fleeting thought. Yet for a while, just for a short while, it will be there, not dark or lonely or brooding, not even solitary but triumphant and commanding for it was shrouded once in that eternal now, the hope and longing and the promise mirrored in the face of a smiling child, the soft, sweet ache holding this land together.

If old man Buck Burroughs could have imagined how farming would be today and someone had asked him about the future of this Delta as he sat in front of the store, waiting to get his mail and talking, he may have looked off for a long time with a stare in the distance, then answered, "Well, I think it can be all right," and in a loud voice he would add, "I cleared some of it. Ah-God-suh, I know it." After thinking awhile, he would add, "You know, we had cotton pretty well worked out once. We knew how to make cotton. A man could buy some land, clear it and pay for it growing cotton and have a good living doing it. But, they done changed things up. You try that now. It takes mules to make cotton and you got to pick it in August and September. Looks like we got a lot of doing and learning yet ahead." He would pick up his reins and drive the buggy off a short distance, then stop his horse and turn back to continue after another pause and a far stare, "Why, we used to keep our own books. These tenants we got now, Ah-God-suh, are keeping the books on us." Then he would add, "And we always brought our seed home from the gin. We grew our diesel fuel, too. Why, there ain't even no cotton buyers now. Where would a man sell his cotton? We used to have two or three in Duncan and I can remember about six cotton offices in Shelby. Cleveland had a whole street full of 'em, enough to keep a four chair barber shop busy and a five story hotel nearly full. Two or three trains a day would stop there, letting them off from Memphis or picking them up. Folks forget it, but we done gone from mules to modules to moons in too short a time. We got some catching up to do." After another long stare in the distance, he might turn and add, "The land's all right. We just got to re-learn what to do with it, how to work it."

The magic of science and the lure of the white fiber, may bring it again to these rolling plains, yet those sturdy people who brought it here, those pioneers who came into this swampy mosquito wilderness, stayed and then turn turned it into a garden, are gone, left to history and to legend, erased as all flesh, by the winds of time. But, they had come here to stay. They built homes, with families. Soon a church was here and shortly afterwards a school, then some law enforcement, and stores, some semblance of commerce, a railroad depot came early.

I remember Daddy talking about this and I had asked him about the differences, between the permanent ones and the later Memphis crowd that did not persevere. He said that those who lasted had always saved part of what they had made and didn't live on borrowed money. They had a good life but in looking back on it he could see that they had never tried to impress anyone and were but rarely impressed themselves.

They never ate their seed corn.

It seemed the survivors had tried to give something back, they educated their children, had permanent homes, they didn't spend it all on themselves, usually very little. They paid their debts. The debts we all owe. The debts to the future.

Still the land—the land is here—the dark, mellow, fecund land, the weeds, the mud, the harvest, the frozen stalks, yielding before an arctic blast, then the smooth, friable fields, green again with the hope of life, all in your vision and compass—the land—that's all that ever was here and those frugal heirs, those who, without greed or avarice, those who do not pirate it, those who will think and sweat, they will survive and endure and enjoy living here, they will reap its generous abundance.

ONE WITH NINEVEH

The Uncle's Tale

Lo, all our pomp of yesterday
Is one with Nineveh and Tyre!

Rudyard Kipling
Recessional

John T. was sitting on the railroad sidetrack platform when I drove up, his feet dangling a yard from the ground. Across the road were the two old, vacant, brick store buildings. It was mid morning, early July, hot, and the humid air was heavy, almost wet on your skin. John T. was sitting there leaning forward, both hands on the platform on each side of him, countering his forward thrust. He had on a white shirt and a wool suit buttoned neatly to the wide part of the lapels. His ample, red tie was tight, causing the skin to bulge out above his collar. I stopped to talk with him and saw his face, smooth and dry as a chalkboard and just as unwrinkled, until he recognized me, when a smooth wave spread over it showing two gold teeth. I asked him what he was doing. He told me he had been over talking to Mr. Bob and was getting ready to go to church down yonder, and he pointed down the road to the south.

There wasn't another human in sight and I had seen none since I came through Shelby and turned onto the gravel road a quarter mile south of where he sat. The gravel road ran by a partially collapsed, three room, shotgun house, once painted a light blue, now faded and dull. Some of the windows were missing and the outhouse behind it already toppled to a cluster of boards on the ground. A hundred yards further were two cinder block, three room houses, only one with a roof and both with doors missing or barely hanging by one lone hinge.

Behind this, sat White Plains Church, squat and low to the ground, splayed out, like a white hen covering a full nest in summer. A twelve foot bell tower stood just to the north. This same church is where Professor Hull went on Sundays and came every weekday for four months each year to teach school. The church will open now only "Second Sunday," their "Pastorial Sunday." Then, at most, three or four cars will be there. The vast swarms have gone. No more crowds outside the church to meet and visit and talk two hours before preaching started. The sharp turn off the gravel, a short distance from the church, once passed John Nelson's store. John's store had been gone fifty years, along with the crowds each Sunday that filled the church yard, then spread out into the road.

John T. had a badge, eight inches in diameter, hanging on a short chain from the buttonhole, high up in his right lapel. The word USHER in bright gold lettering was spread across the entire width of it. As he leaned forward, the badge hung out away from this chest and swung side to side a little as he moved or spoke. It hung there, striking and impressive, glaring as the Kaiser's insignia and was the keystone atop the white shirt and coat, the tie, and the gold teeth. It was authentic and authoritative. With it, he was a valid, bona fide officer and high Deacon of the church. He knew it, too. As he told me, "Dis badge means I's a genuine Ersher. I tells 'em whar to sit." John T. was there to do just that. Though there was no need now to place the eight or ten people in the big open church.

I chatted with John T. a short time, his shining, grinning face bright and smooth, still dry as powder, then drove on around toward Uncle Bob's house. It sat there alone and quiet, a short distance away in a grove of pecan trees, at the end of an asphalt road.

Just to the south of the house, in what is now a pasture and a twenty acre ancient pecan orchard, you can still see several small mounds of partially buried bricks, the last visible evidence of fireplaces and chimneys once warming a thirty room, two-storied boarding house, twenty-five years old when he and his family moved there. The wide porches on each floor facing the railroad toward the east were free of any sun from noon until the following morning.

Built during the 1880s, shortly after the railroad came, to house the visiting stockholders, the owners of Hushpuckena Creek Pecan Company, a vast orchard extending to the south and east from where it sat. Not a hundred yards from the railroad depot, they had a place to come, from which to view, in comfort, their immense holdings, a fifteen hundred acre pecan orchard. From a second story front porch perspective, the scene would be at least a mile and a half toward the south and to the east, a much longer and more hopeful and less troubling view than Lee had, when studying the valley, across which he would send Picket's Division. All of the investors were Yankees, most with profits gathered during the Civil War and anxious to invest in a successful enterprise. None, more inviting than the fertile lands of the south. The most productive of these, the warm, loamy Mississippi Delta.

The promoters of this project were a small group from Memphis. They had bought the land from the railroad for fifty cents an acre and resold it to the pecan company's stockholders for around five hundred, plus legal fees, but with sixteen trees per acre, the stockholders could easily have their money returned and a huge profit after only a few years of production.

All of the company's stationery and their literature documented and confirmed this. At the top of each sheet they had placed a picture of a giant tree, probably an oak, on which an artist had painted hundreds of pecans, some as big, almost, as coconuts. There it was for all to see, no mistaking it. The soon to be bountiful production, of the Hushpuckena Creek Pecan Company. The Yankees had heard about the rich, alluvial, warm Delta land, fertile and readily fruitful, mellow and friable, capable of producing anything. Those who had never heard about it were told, and with the pecan native here, then grafted, these trees would soon rain giant pecans. There were the pictures to prove it. They easily oversold their first issue of stock, but that didn't matter. Who would ever know? They just filled out more certificates and continued offering paper for Yankees' money.

The venture seemed to prosper for awhile. Fifteen hundred acres were set out in pecans and investors were brought down in groups of fifteen or twenty to stay for a week or two. While here, there was a schedule of activities. They rode around the orchard on horseback or in buggies, which took several days, or went on fishing trips about a mile away, along the banks of a deep hole in a sharp bend on Hushpuckena Creek. Some would get horses from the livery stable and ride for miles toward the east or back toward the river, looking at the farming operations, which were, with few exceptions, only small clearings by a dirt road. There was a big steam powered saw mill with extensive logging operations along a dummy railroad line made with wooden rails and pulled by single file mules walking on planks between the rails. The lines extended east to the Sunflower River with branches both to the north and south. Sections of a huge, gigantic cypress log, mountainous and solid, were sent to the Chicago World's Fair during the summer months of 1893 and there were logs being brought into the mill on a daily basis. Some of the orchard investors later bought land here in one hundred sixty to six hundred and forty acre blocks. The acreage today still bearing their names.

After several years of apparent little growth of the trees and no pecan production, the visiting investors became fewer and fewer. Some trees were nearly fifteen years old before there was any production and by then the Yankees had enough of the warm, luxuriant Delta summers and the cold mud of winter and the visitations stopped. For years after that, the boarding house was rented to travelers and workmen, some with families.

For about half the summer each year from mid May until after the Fourth of July, about cotton picking time, chicken fights were held just across the railroad from the boarding house. There were ten to twelve, six by six foot pits dug into the ground and at peak times each day simultaneous fights were in session in each pit, where a pair of long spurred game cocks, bred to fight and win or until death, faced each other in mortal combat. Many a pair of panting lungs were infected with the spores of histoplasmosis while trying to breathe life back into a bleeding, fatally wounded gladiator. Enthusiasts from western Kansas to New Orleans were here. Some of the bunch, high in their spirits one night, it was later said, let a lamp fall on the floor, burning down the boarding house. Staying there until the 1920s, it had well served its purpose.

Presently, only about twenty acres of the trees are left, though for forty years the vast orchard was there. The spreading acres, unbowed and fruitful, cool and restful, producing more than their original cost each year. The few survivors, now bent, stooped, and battered, moribund, disease stricken and old, old even for wood, left to decay, and to ice storms and to the wind. They are productive no more and the earth will soon claim the last of them. These few broken trees are the only remnants of the Hushpuckena Creek Pecan Company, once fifteen hundred acres of giant, graceful trees, prolific and beautiful, furled in their night green, breeze tossed, shimmering color, south and east from the boarding house where only a few earth covered bricks, mark its once lofty promise, with not a hint or a trace to recall its illusory purpose. No memory, no fading stock certificates, nothing. The earth holding forever its secrets.

∞

When I went into the house, Uncle Bob's sitter told me to go on back, he might be dozing, but John T. had been there a short time before and he probably wasn't asleep. Besides, she added, he had just had her "back there looking for a pair of new shoes, he happened to think about, that he had worn to Christine's wedding," a niece, now almost eighty years old, who had gotten married during early World War II.

I walked on back to the big, high ceilinged, sixteen foot square room with double windows on two sides and saw him lying on the bed. The same iron bed where he lay for seven weeks in 1918 with the Spanish flu and again in 1946 for four weeks with the flu again, but this time not the Spanish variety. In 1918, during the weekends, Daddy slept in that same bed with him, then each Monday morning he got on the four o'clock train and went back to Bolivar County Agricultural High School in Cleveland. Slept with him each weekend for seven weeks and never ran a fever. He and Daddy had slept in that same room since 1914. Daddy moved out when he got married in 1929.

I saw him lying there in his bed, ninety four years old, his head supported on pillows, neck frail and wrinkled as an unfeathered nest bird. His shaven face placid with cheeks slightly sunken, almost wax like, close short cropped white hair. His form causing only a slender bulge in the spread as it easily flowed over him with a gentle ascent, then across in a minor ripple back to the plain surface of the opposite side. From a distance of twelve feet there was hardly any curvature at all in the smooth surface of the bed. The straight fingered hands clasped across his chest were not gnarled or angulated, only slightly coarsened and narrow and reached strong and direct with a tremulous, though slower, grasp. His face old like whitened, weathered rock or stone, did not appear drawn and tired. The sharp profile was angled against the sun brightened window. There was no defeat or surrender or despair in it, only a relaxed endurance and persistent perseverance against fate and irrevocable mortality. I called his name several times before he answered. He must have been dreaming, for he turned and, facing an open window, spoke several times in a loud voice, as if he thought I was outside, before realizing I was in the room with him. Although his vision is faded and almost gone, he remains alert and converses well. He stays at home now, has several sitters who alternate shifts staying with him.

In about 1990 he awoke one morning and said he didn't feel good and never went back to his store. A store that had been opened every day since it was built in about 1908. His father bought it and operated it for years until Uncle Bob and my daddy operated it and used it for a commissary for their farm.

I asked him how he was getting along and how his sitters were doing, just something for him to hear my voice again and get me located within the room. He replied that Loraine had gone to the hospital, but Mrs. Watson was still preaching. "Does she still preach pretty good?" I asked. "She preaches good to Loraine and me. She's even gone to carryin' a Bible and preaching day and night. I think she's lookin' for a church to pastor. She used to preach to Loraine all the time, but since she's gone, she preaches to me now. Her congregation has been cut in half." "She doesn't bother you, does she?" I asked him. "No, she dud'n bother me a lot. I cut her off when I get ready." "How do you do that?" "I tell 'er that she don't know what she's talkin' about, had'n read far enough over in the Bible yet, not nearly far enough to get her text right. She needs to study the scriptures a little more. Then, I might even tell her that she needs to read further on over in the Bible like I have, on over in Paul and Matthew. That usually shuts her down and she takes her Bible and goes on over in her room and starts reading again."

He reached over in the direction of the bedside table, his hand then feeling across it toward a glass, took a sip, and with a short breath situated it back in exactly the same spot and continued.

"You know, she started that mess about the time Jimmy Swaggart started preachin'. She's gotten worse ever since." He hesitated a short while, gazed toward the window, then turned back. "Aw, she's born again, ya know, and will tell ya about it in a minute, stops people on the street she don't even know and tells 'em. She listens to that Brother Hall now somewhere up in Tennessee." He gazed upward a moment, as if he were looking toward the ceiling, then added, "You know, that Brother Swaggart wuz a pretty good preacher. 'Course, he could'n let women alone, but that did'n seem to bother his preachin' any. He could preach, sing too, had a good voice, and he played the piano. Did some of it all, just a walking church service, preaching, praying, singing, and piano playing. I saw 'im preach once 'til he gave out, just wore down, then held his Bible straight up over his head as far as he reach, nearly up out of sight, and started skippin' and dancin' across the stage, singin' and hollerin' 'til he was outta breath, completely choked down, then sat down at that piano and started playin'. He rested a minute, then sang. Sang a pretty good song, too. He's one of the best shows on there and I think he's the one that got her started. But, she's born again now. She can go at it herself. Seems like there's somethin' about that Bible that just makes 'em all wanta preach."

I asked him about Loraine, his other sitter. I'd heard that

she went to Jackson to the hospital for an operation. "Well, you know, she did'n have an operation," he answered and he turned, fixing his unseeing, sightless eyes directly toward me. Then, he added, "She had gotten onto beer and crack cocaine." He paused a moment, then continued, "Yessir, beer and crack cocaine, and had to go down to the rehab in Jackson to dry out." "When did you know that?" I asked him. "She was here every day and I never thought she was doin' nothin' like that. She sure fooled me. Why, she was at the rehab dryin' out and I thought she was gone to take an operation." I told him that he should have gotten Mrs. Watson on her, preaching to her, then maybe she could have helped her get off the stuff and would not have had to go to Jackson. "I had forgotten," he said, "that that's what she had been doing. Why, Mrs. Watson was her trouble. She preached to her so hard and so much that Loraine got scared and when she got over into Revelations and started preaching that to her, she got to where she would'n leave the house after dark. She got here about eight in the mornin' and left at four in the afternoon. That's when Loraine started carryin' a Bible herself and would sit there all day readin' it. Why, Mrs. Watson just preached to her too hard," he continued, "That cocaine was the only thing she could get to lighten Mrs. Watson up off of her. She just wore her out. Then, too, the Bible must'a read better to her when she was under that beer and crack cocaine. I'm goin' to have to keep Mrs. Watson off of her when she gets back," he continued.

∞

I asked him if they had ever had a church in Hushpuckena. "Yeah, we had preachin' regular here for a long time when I was a boy. Over in the old schoolhouse. Had a preacher from Shelby here two or three Sundays a month, then one would come from Duncan to fill in the rest. We had one of 'em every Sunday. In the summer, long 'bout lay-by time, one would come here and hold a revival. We had one here one summer from

Port Gibson. I can see him now. I was about twelve." He turned, as if gazing toward the window, and after a pause, slowly continued, "I believe he was better than Jimmy Swaggart. He'd make the windows rattle. Some of 'em looked like they wanted to cry when he preached. Mr. Embry, who had'n heard a preacher in twenty years, stood straight up, right in the middle of some of his preachin' and started hollerin'.

That preacher combed his hair straight back, had a little pair of glasses set out on the end of his nose, a big pot belly, looked the spittin' image of Bilbo. Preached here all week. Then, that next Sunday carried twelve or fourteen of us down to the creek and baptized us all."

He seemed to be staring at the ceiling now, but he hesitated a moment, then turned toward the light of the window and after awhile forged on, telling the story in a slow, steady voice, like something that had happened last week. "Me and ya Daddy, Papa Granny, were in the bunch he baptized. Let's see, who else was? Mr. Taylor, old Falkner. I think A. D. Murphree was in it. A gang of us. Took all Sunday morning. Had a crowd. The bank was lined. He got started early when it was cool. But, it was nearly dinnertime when he got through.

Toward the end, he had a great big fellow who worked in the Allen Store. He nearly drowned him. He came out of the creek and he had to lay on the bank awhile to catch his breath. Another thirty seconds would'a got 'im. That lasted on several more years. I think they baptized about everybody around here.

One summer they got our law, Uncle Billy Wooten." He paused and turned toward the window again when he said that name. "They say that was the only time in forty years that he did'n have his pistol on him. Took it off, laid it on the bank just before he waded out in the creek. Uncle Billy wasn't very tall, only about five feet. Standing next to the preacher, he was in water up to his chin. Preacher baptized him. He waded out, picked up his pistol, strapped it on as he came out, over his wet gown. Never stopped. Got on his horse and rode on home. I think he shot a tenant stealing hay the next day.

That went on until after World War I. Then in the twenties kinda played out." "It must have been that dollar cotton in 1919 that slowed it up," I asked. "Yeah, and that six cent cotton the next year," he said. "That helped phase it out and all that bootleg whiskey finally just killed it. But, they graveled the roads in '23 and with a few cars around, some of 'em here would go to Duncan or Shelby to a revival. Aw, a revival would draw 'em all right. That was the thing to do in the summer. Go to revival. I imagine there was more courtin' goin' on at revivals than anywhere else. 'Course, we had picnics and ball games to go to then."

He seemed to take a deep breath and, after a brief lull, continued with a slight grin. "You know, that was the only thing Papa would let us leave the field for. A ballgame or a good picnic. On the Fourth, we had one that lasted all day long. A game in the morning and another one that afternoon and the best picnic you ever went to. We had a good place to have a picnic and a ballgame, down there in the bottom, close to the creek. Had us a good diamond, smoothed off, and plenty of shade behind it. You know, a good picnic is all right and we had some good ones here. You remember, your Daddy had some good ones here when ya'll were little. We'd get about a hundred pounds of catfish from over on the river and Buck would come down and get his fire started and start cookin' about two o'clock and we'd eat then about four." He paused another moment, then continued, "I 'member goin' to a good picnic down at, I believe it was, Leroy Percy Park on one Fourth. They'd always have a big thing down there. Had plenty of good shade and a speaker's platform. Had politicians from around over the state down talking.

That Fourth, the politicians started talking about noontime and there was one, on the platform talking 'til about two o'clock. I had noticed a little tiny fella, looked like a little bird, sitting over on the edge of the speaker's platform. Had on a coat in July, rumpled all up. He did'n do any talkin'. Just the politicians. When they were finished, we all drifted over to the fish tables and started gettin' our plates full. I noticed after awhile a few people were drifting back toward the speaker's platform. I looked over there and saw that little fella, in that rumpled up coat, up on the platform talking. I walked on over and, first thing you know, the whole crowd had drifted back over there to listen to 'im." He paused another moment, then continued, "You know, that little ole fella made one of the best speeches, I believe, I've ever heard. Made a better speech than all those politicians put together. Didn't talk but about thirty minutes, but everybody left the fish tables and went over there and listened to 'im." I asked him, "Bob, what did he talk about? What did he tell ya'll?" He hesitated a moment and then said, "You know, I don't remember what he was talkin' about, but he made one of the best speeches I ever heard." I asked him if he was a politician. He seemed to gaze toward the light of the window, as if looking out across his yard and afterwards he said, "Naw, I don't think he was a politician." He hesitated again, then added, "But, that little fella made the damndest speech, I b'lieve I ever heard. We all hated when he quit, just stood there a minute before we went back to the picnic."

Then, he slowly turned and looked toward me, but I knew that he didn't see me. His eyes only turned in my direction and, though sightless, he must have seen something far off and distant, and remembered, too. "When the revivals played out, did they continue to have church here?" I asked. "Yeah," he pressed on, "we had church service in the old schoolhouse once or twice a month when a preacher would come by and spend Saturday night here with somebody, wherever he had heard the eatin' was pretty good. You know, they got a communication ring, like the Tong, or the Brotherhood, to pass all that along. Then, after a short while, they made the schoolhouse into a residence and that ended the church and the preaching.

Later on, we had a Sunday school over in the store. We sent off to the Southern Baptists and got the Sunday school books and song books, had Eva for a teacher. You remember her,

Aldine's wife. I remember the first few Sundays she taught. Her mouth got so dry she could hardly say a word. But, she kept at it and got pretty good. In fact, she was real good, better than a lotta preachers. Prepared her lesson three or four hours each Saturday afternoon."

He paused again, a long time before he continued. Then turned and seemed to focus his sightless eyes on me and added, "You know, it's surprising, the talent and ability some people have and you never know it 'til they're in a special situation and called on to use it. Then, it all comes out." He paused again, then said, "Your Daddy was always like that.

Dollie was in it, too, and all of her bunch. And Dollie led the singing. She had a good voice, too. Never took a lesson, as far as I know. Her Daddy, Mr. Feather, liked to sing and he must have started her early. She'd get eight or ten of 'em singing, each with a songbook, of course, to keep 'em together and it resonated around in that big store, sounded like a huge church." "Bob," I asked him, "do you remember the time Harmon began singing and just couldn't quit?" He seemed to stare toward the ceiling again, hesitated a moment, then laughed, "Yeah, we had to lead him out around back of the store and run water on him to get him to hush."

"We had a good program for several years," he continued, "getting mail at the post office, 'Hushpuckena Sunday School.' 'Course, Eva being the post mistress and the teacher, got all the Sunday school literature and songbooks, then passed them out, and we got the bill for the books, and so forth, in our box. But, it rocked along pretty good. Lasted several years. We had twenty or more each Sunday.

Then, one Sunday morning, a car pulled up out front and a Brother Barrett from somewhere down around Shaw, said he was some kind of missionary, showed up and wanted to start preaching, two Sundays a month. Well, we talked to him and he seemed all right. Hadn't been to school much. But, we thought he might do for us. We knew we couldn't get one of those well trained preachers to come preach to us in that store.

We told him we would let him know, but the next Sunday he was there, ready to preach. Did preach there in the store. He hung around long enough to let us know that he wanted twenty-five dollars a Sunday and would be there every other Sunday. I think Gene gave him the twenty-five dollars and he took off.

That's when some of our crowd quit coming. I don't think many of them like preachers anyway. Of course, that broke up the Sunday School, but the preacher kept coming. Eventually, he just preached it right down to nothing. The last time he came was during the winter. Must have been February. He had just started only several years before."

Uncle Bob gazed toward the window again, then continued. "We had a big fire in that side room in the "Chinaman" store, sitting around the heater when he came in. We weren't looking for him that Sunday. It was cold and the crowd had already about played out. Me and Gene and Will Gardner, one of the tenants, were in there sitting on Co-Cola cases. I think Sonny was there. The preacher got up there by that heater and preached anyway. Preached nearly an hour to just the three of us and Sonny. I think Gene gave him five dollars when he got through. He had been looking at some Brookfield sausage in that ice box so hard and bragged on it so much, he gave him a pound box of that. Yessir, five dollars and a pound box of Brookfield sausage for a Sunday morning's preaching. He didn't come back. We didn't hear from him anymore." He paused again, longer this time, with a gaze toward the light of the window, then slowly continued, still with a clear, strong voice, "You know, that was something. He came up here and broke up the Sunday School, and we had a good one. Then, the preaching played out and him supposed to be a missionary of some sort.

While he was here, though, we did have some pretty good revivals during the summer." I asked him, "Bob, where did you hold a revival here?" He was quick to answer, "In that 'Chinaman' store. We had it fixed up, painted white inside, like new. Seventy-five or eighty chairs. Might have had even a hundred. Twelve or fourteen, hundred and fifty watt light bulbs hanging from the ceiling. Aw, it was lit up like the Kate Adams under a full head of steam. We had some good crowds, too. Fifteen or twenty from Duncan, about that many from Shelby, and the country was full of folks, all this bunch around here. It was usually in July. It was hot. We had a fan or two in there. It was all right." Then, another lull and a short rest.

He had been gesturing some, but his hands were now at his side. As he turned, he seemed to be looking directly at me again. I encouraged him to continue. "I remember Bill Evans from over on Sugar Hill. He would always come. The first night he had on a dress shirt with the collar open. No tie. But, a big tie pin, one of those 1920 Al Capone pins stuck in his shirt. I think Mrs. Evans had put that on him, in place of a tie, to let the people know he would have worn one if it hadn't been so hot.

Brother Barrett usually got some youngster just starting out to come preach the revival. The local preacher would always do that, get some outside preacher to come to preach a revival." There was a short pause again and his voice faded, as his head turned down a moment, then it surged back. "I reckon that's because with an outside preacher the people don't know him, don't suspect him of nothing, no reason for him not to tell the truth. That summer he got Calvin Hughes, Bill Hughes' boy from over there out from Duncan, to come down and preach. I think Calvin was trying to get off whiskey, had took up preaching, and we thought we might try him." The tone of his voice changed a little as he turned toward me again and continued. "If a man can't grow cotton here, there's not much left for him to do, except maybe clerk in a store or sell insurance. Then, sometimes a few of 'em will take up preachin' and that's what he had done. He was supposed to be pretty good. He had preached around in the country some. So we took a chance on him." He turned toward the window again, hesitated a moment, then added, "I think that was the last one we had."

∞

Through the window and the trees of his front yard, he would have seen the "Chinaman" store, had his vision been intact, and it seems, even now, that somehow he did, for after awhile he started talking about what he saw seventy-five years before, when the revivals were held in the schoolhouse, before the Chinamen had arrived even. The building then had been a drugstore. That's what it was built for.

The shelves then were rowed with patent medicines of all varieties. Sweet Spirits of Niter, Turpentine, Sloan's liniment, aspirin, Lydia E. Pinkham's, and a myriad of others. Cocaine was there with laudanum, morphine, and paregoric, its camphorated cousin. Anodynes in powders, liquid, or pills. There to assuage the pains of implacable mortality and the restricting walls of awakened consciousness, all later removed by Mr. Harrison and the National Congress.

There were few, if any, addicts at the time and no drug problem in the entire area. Even though, with only a quarter, they could gain ready access to any of the poppies' and cocas' favors. But, people had to work to eat.

Blocks of camphor, potassium nitrate with its whispered, but false, legendary consequences, though believed to be in the water or food, it may doom an outing of the impressionable and receptive. Tinctures of all kinds added their medicinal pungency to the store.

Abe Plough had several of the most sought after and best sellers there. His St. Joseph aspirin made in Memphis and first peddled there on the street along with his "Camphorated Healing Oil," a mixture of camphor and cottonseed oil, were now on the shelves and would rapidly move out. He also had a popular "female tonic," but his best seller was G-22-23, a mixture of quinine in a low dose, only for the bitter taste, and potassium iodide, then used to produce more phlegm when coughing, giving the illusion of coughing up and ridding the lungs of any disease, be it TB or lung fever. This came with a bold guarantee, printed in easy to read letters right on the front of the tall, orange and white, nine inch box housing an eight ounce corked bottle:

"THIS MEDICINE IS BENEFICIAL IN ALL CONDITIONS IN WHICH A MEDICINE OF THIS TYPE IS INDICATED." There it was for all to see. It had to be good. Groves Chill Tonic, five grain quinine capsules at fifty cents a dozen, there for the yearly bouts of chills, rigors, and fevers. Dr. Carter's Little Liver Pills, Black Draught, Epsom Salts, Castor Oil, and the tooth jarring toxic, calomel, a mercury compound, had their section. There were cough medicines and worm pills and a choice of preparations for scabies, skin fungus, and any skin infection. A "calmative" or "normative," made with a dab of quinine and heavy doses of potassium bromide were on the shelves. Miles Nervine and numerous other nerve tonics were placed with them. The effectiveness of medicine was directly proportional to the bitterness of its taste. Iron tonics and Cocoa Quinine were there for children along with worm medicines. If it said "tonic" on the box and had a bitter taste, it had to be good and the patient usually survived it. Probably few of the drugs helped any, except the quinine and iron, then only if taken in a proper dosage. Of course, opiates afforded tremendous relief, to calm the agonizing terror and expedite the passage into a painless, euphoric, somnolence until the final passage was made.

Fred Grisham was the first to operate the drugstore, but he had no pharmacist. Didn't need one. He could sell anything he wanted and those country doctors didn't write prescriptions. I bet there weren't two pharmacists in the entire Delta. They would have starved depending upon prescriptions. Fred had him a good store, though. Sold cosmetics and perfumes and the usual drugstore items. Anything you wanted but clothes and groceries or hardware. Later on, he had a soda fountain. Did a good business. Made a living at it.

Papa's second store in the town, and his last one, which is there now, next to the Chinaman store, was built of brick about 1903 and he bought it from Mr. Burroughs around 1916. The store is eighty feet long and about twenty-five to thirty feet wide. There were four others here then, long frame buildings.

The others sold mostly groceries, but Papa had just about anything you needed. Kept five clerks busy on Saturday. There were shoes of all varieties and boots, leather and rubber. Ladies, kid, leather shoes with spoon heels, black, white and brown ones. Children's shoes of all sorts. There was nowhere to get any unless you got on the train and went to Memphis, and this was a big area here, from the Mississippi River to the Sunflower. There were all kinds of patent medicines and any form of tobacco. Groceries filled the next shelves, and in drawers under counters, were dried beans and peas. Salt meat and bacon lay on tables. Sausages hung on long racks overhead. Flour and meal in forty-eight pound sacks and in barrels, vinegar in wooden barrels with a wooden pump, spices, from cloves to nutmeg in jars added their aroma. There was any kind of soap or detergent. Toward the back of the building, he had mule collars and hames and shoulder pads, bridles, trace chains, coils of rope, and hardware, anything made of iron, for a farm, from nails to bolts to stoves. Shotgun shells and Winchester bullets were stacked in their place. Pots and pans, washtubs and washing boards were rowed on counters, cutlery, and dishes in shelves and on counters. Then, a long wall of shelves and counters with clothes, from overalls, jumpers, khaki pants and shirts, to stockings, dresses, bolts of cloth, and step-ins, anything to wear, even union suits, and head protectors of all sorts. Handkerchiefs, arm and leg garters, bed sheets, towels and blankets had a place.

All types of overlay and wrappings for protecting and hiding, covering, and enhancing the human form. There were lotions and balms, colognes and sachet, even powders on the shelves to add gloss and intensify and augment an attracting smile.

With all of this, including soaps of many strengths and flavors, even perfumes galore, something basic and vital was missing. There were no deodorants or antiperspirants and bathing was only a weekly chore. Yet, girls were pretty and sooner or later could be attracted to boys, scent and all, so their efforts were never an exercise in futility. Maybe one effluvium canceled the other, like two dissimilar particles. They met, exchange a photon, collide and disintegrate into myriad quanta of energy. Both encounters were of about the same significance, both bound still by the second law, sure as the theory of multiple small dilutions. Some creatures flaunt their scent, but man alone, among all the animals, tries to hide his and is the only one that needs to.

Hundreds of stores like this were dotted across the Delta, with probably more than a hundred in this county alone. They supplied the total needs of the labor force and most of the needs of the entire populace. They were in towns, at crossroads, at plantation headquarters, anywhere eight or ten people might gather. To get there in winter would require a horse or a team of four to six mules pulling a wagon. One of the mules might fall and drown before you could get back home. A long winter could mean a big portion of Sir Walter Scott, Emerson, and William Thackery. A few even, may winter with Balzac or Dostoevski, and the Bard, except for the occasional party lasting sometimes several weeks or a week in Memphis.

Yafee and Rosen had a big dry goods store just to the south of Papa's. They had come to this Delta from eastern Poland in the 1880s and were peddlers for fifteen or twenty years until they opened that store. As peddlers, they had been supplied by one of the Brethren, a big dry goods merchant in St. Louis. They had walked this Delta from one end to the other, many times, selling mostly to tenants. When they opened their store, they brought their families over and they lived in the opposite end of it. The families did not get along for some reason and in only a year or two, one of them moved out. The one that stayed, however, kept the same name, Yafee and Rosen, and operated the store until the Depression, when he left. That Depression scattered lots of them, not just people from eastern Poland, either.

To the south of that store stood Papa's gin, later operated by your Daddy. Old man Jeffries was in that gin along with Papa, Mr. Taylor, and Joe Yates. They all finally died out and your

Daddy bought it. Then, in the early fifties, south of that, he built that new one. A short distance away was White Plain Church.

John Nelson had a store, close by there. I think his Daddy had been a slave. He had a boy, Shelby, who could play a trumpet smooth as anything you ever heard, better than any of them at the Peabody, or on those river showboats out of New Orleans. He would sit down there, on that porch on Sunday evening and play that horn. I can almost hear him now. It had that high pitched trumpet sound, but it was soft and mellow. It would flow out across town, smooth as the water on a windless pond, not a ripple in it. Sometimes he would play it all Sunday evening, on until after sundown. There would always be a crowd gather there to listen to him. Somebody on one of the trains, that stopped here one Sunday, heard him. He went back to Memphis and told Handy. Handy sent for him. They said he played with Handy until his band broke up. We never did hear where he went after that. He was good, could beat these little old things tooting horns around here and on the TV. He just picked it up himself. I think his daddy got that horn for him, when he was a little boy, out of a pawn shop in Memphis. Bought it for about three dollars.

Just beyond John Nelson's store, down on the lower end, several shacks and lean-to's wandered on back in the field. Some of the tenants went to these juke joints on Saturday nights, where the roar would rival Beale Street before Mr. Crump's time. These joints were never entered by anyone else except the law. The field just before you got to the Nelson's store, later occupied by a gin, was empty then, except for an ancient small cemetery and a tiny church in one corner.

This same field was just across the railroad from the Pecan Company's boarding house and is the site where the chicken fights were held. These fights would usually end by the Fourth of July. But, one summer, long after the Fourth, the fights were still raging, with a fluster and a fury far surpassing anything seen in the past. That year there were rogues and gamblers here from six states and invariably fights would erupt daily. With crowds getting bigger and wilder, with no end in sight, some of the citizens sent a messenger by train, down to Cleveland to inform the sheriff, and try to get some relief.

The sheriff, Nick Edwards, was here on the next train. With badge and pistol prominently displayed, he made the rounds of the stores, shook everybody's hand, assured them he would break up the violent rowdiness and rapidly proceeded toward the yelling crowd. Two weeks later, they sent for a deputy to come get Nick.

The town had a post office early, shortly after the railroad came through. Papa's store was enlisted for that purpose, when he was appointed postmaster during Teddy Roosevelt's administration. Later, a frame, cypress shingled building, about twenty feet square, placed just to the north of the Chinaman store served as a postal dispensary. A mail crane across the road from it stood there for years and boldly endured, poised upright, cocked like a hair triggered pistol with its arms outstretched when holding a bag of mail, eight or nine times a day. Spring loaded and ready, waiting to hand a seventy mile an hour train, the bag, which would dematerialize and instantly disappear, leaving a new bag tumbling along the embankment. The mail crane was a clever contraption, as ingenious and simple, for its time, and necessary as Archimedes' screw or Marconi's wireless. Like Columbus standing that egg on end, it's simple when somebody shows you how. It gave every small town and hamlet ready access to daily mail service with any civilized spot on earth, equal to New York or London. A man's thoughts would be sent anywhere he wished, for less than a nickel, as accurately as they could be pressed onto paper. Early, the telegraph was an unbelievable God-send, too. Forty or fifty people gathered around the depot one summer night to hear a Jack Dempsey prize fight, blow by blow, as it happened in New York, hollered out by the depot agent inside.

A lumber company was directly up the street. Lumber and building materials brought there by the train and moved out on a wagon pulled by mules and in the winter by oxen. Later, a service station was close by and a small grocery store operated by the new owner of the lumber company, Jack and Ada Sikes. On further to the north, early, were two huge general mercantile stores, made of cypress boards and shingled roofs. Seventy feet long, with rooms along each side for storage of goods or space to rent out for clerks, or bookkeepers or anyone else who needed a place to sleep for a week or a month. Close by the Jeffries store stood a two story Victorian home, where the store owner and his family lived. D. J. Allen owned the next store. He had bought the old Pecan Company's land and farmed about twelve hundred acres of it in cotton. The livery stable was on up, next to the creek, along with a boarding house, where a number of the clerks, bookkeepers, and farm managers lived, and any others without wives. There was always a crowd there at noon to eat. Across the railroad to the west were several stores. Papa's original store was there, but had been converted to house several tenant families. Murphree Brothers gin, later run by Leland Oil Works, stood a short distance, farther to the south. A big blacksmith shop to the west, down a narrow dirt road, was a short distance away. It kept Mr. Embry busy, shoeing horses and mules, sharpening plow points, and repairing any farm implement, wagons, and tools that had not survived prolonged and repetitive use. Mr. Embry was also a master wheel-wright. He was known as the best in the county. No spoke or wheel rim placed by him ever loosened. When he repaired a wheel, it was said to be better than new from the factory.

Papa's first house in Hushpuckena was only a short distance from this store with a big cistern in the front yard. Daddy told of a time about 1907 when he was three years old, playing with one of his sisters and several other children, when they looked up and saw an automobile coming over the railroad crossing. All of them scattered like a covey of flushed quails. Being much younger than the others, he could not run as fast. His sister ran back, picked him up and got to the house as soon as the others.

A Chinaman tried later to operate a store on that side of town. At the time there was already a Chinaman store where the drugstore had been. The first Chinaman there got the Tong, to send a soldier to make the later arrival move. The intruding Chinaman left in haste. A dentist followed the chinaman with an office and his living quarters in the building. He was known to poach eggs, in his coffee when boiling and may have introduced café ovum to the Delta. It faded rapidly here, but not before being taken up by chefs in New Orleans.

A young doctor came in 1908, Dr. James Leland Brookshire. He graduated from medical school at Vanderbilt University and spent two years, as long as he could, as a house officer at St. Thomas' Hospital in Nashville. He was probably the best trained physician in the Delta at that time. He had learned to type the diplococcus, gotten from a patient's blood tinged frothy sputum. The diplococcus was identified with a microscope and typed with specific horse serum, observing, numerous times, all night, with his microscope, which serum caused the capsule of the diplococcus to swell. Then, that type, specific serum could be given to the patient and increased his meager chance of survival. But, when here, he had no serum and he could not get any. He had to treat pneumonia with a mustard plaster and hope, as was done prior to Pasteur. He had learned to do a cesarean section, but there was no operating room. He had done many appendectomies in Nashville, but he had no anesthesia here. Those were sent by train to Memphis or Vicksburg, but when they left here, they had usually ruptured. Since he could not do a cesarean section, his skills with forceps, though very good when he came, rapidly improved. He knew how to dose the leaves of the foxglove, digitalis, and when to prescribe it, but he had to buy the dry leaf and weigh and make his own pills.

Even though training in one of the best hospitals in the country, he chose to ride a horse five miles into the woods on a cold, rainy night, to deliver a baby in a tenant's cabin, and go into the same cabin the next July, to sit in a rank, hundred and ten degree, airless room, on a cane bottomed chair, with the same child, now somewhat longer, but with parchment like skin, emaciated and marasmic, desiccated by two weeks of explosive, profuse diarrhea, to sit there with nothing to offer him, save a small dose of opium powder, while the mother tried hopelessly to get him to drink some sweetened broth, which he had refused for a week. Then, there all day and night, after inserting a rubber tube into his stomach, dripping the same broth into the shrunken, mummified little body, still and lifeless, until long after all signs of a heartbeat and any effort at respiration had been expelled from it. Then, sit helplessly in that same room, the next summer with the child's four-year-old sister and watch, as her high fever, distended abdomen and rectal bleeding, unresponsive to alum and water flushes, progressed to delirium and general coma and she died of the typhoid bacillus.

Old man Buck Burroughs sent a rider in, early one morning, to have the new doctor come out and see him. Mr. Burroughs was well known in the community. The doctor knew this and wanted to make a good impression. He got on his horse and went out, quickly as he could. When he walked in, he saw Mr. Burroughs sitting there on several cushions, his forehead drawn down with a deep scowl on his face, and he soon saw that a big hole was cut out in the bottom of the old man's chair. The doctor walked in with a serious, grim expression on his face. He knew he had to make a good impression. He quickly asked Mr. Burroughs about his trouble. The old man looked at him a minute, then replied, "Doctor, you must have hemorrhoid trouble." "No sir," he said. "Why would you say that?" Mr. Burroughs gazed toward a window awhile, then slowly answered. "Well, a young doctor needs that kind of trouble." Then, after another lull, he added, "He needs it, ah God, suh, 'cause it'll give a man a grave forethought of consideration and a deep air of concern." The doctor carefully examined him, even listening to his heart and chest, but only after he had applied a thick red ointment, heavily laced with cocaine. Mr. Burroughs was feeling better, even when the young doctor left. His scowl had gone, stripped away by the red ointment. In two or three days he was back in his buggy, no cushions, bouncing along in no pain, telling everybody he saw what a good doctor he had. The young doctor's practice took off after that.

Later that day, Dr. Brookshire was called out to see another patient. Always, a rider was sent in to get him. He quickly got his bag and followed the rider out, about three miles, to a three room shack. Lying there in the July heat, on a cotton sack, shuck mattress, black with sweat and grime, in a ten foot square room, a 35-year-old man lay, rolling in agony and holding his hand on his back and pressing hard in his right flank, sweat rolling off of him, in marble size drops, big enough to hit the floor and splatter. An exhausted, almost toothless woman was fanning him with an old newspaper torn from the wall. Her hair, once blond, was a burnt brown now, twisted into wet ropes, hanging thinly to her shoulders. Four, wide eyed children, standing around the room and two neighbors seated close by, one offering him a drink. "Go ahead and take it, Elzy," she said. "With all that sweatin' you're doin', you need some more water." The young doctor took only three steps across the room to his patient. The path was parted through the sweating crowd and he sat in a chair close by the bedside.

After a brief story of his pain, which included an account of passing bloody urine, he knew the man had a kidney stone. He quickly gave him a half grain of morphine. He had dissolved the tiny white tablet in a syringe before he left his office, as he knew he would not find any clean water in the cabin. In less than ten minutes, Elzy's thrashing and pitching and rolling about had noticeably slowed.

There was very little in the room. A fireplace with cold ashes in it, seeing no heat since the previous winter, a small table with some food still on it, covered with flies, a wooden bucket partially filled with water. A few chairs were scattered around the room and a homemade box, half full of some kind of clothing, over in a corner.

After a short time, Elzy's eyes closed as if he might sleep, but then he sat straight up in his bed and, looking around the room, he called out, demanding in a loud voice, "Somma ya'll pay that doctor." Nobody made any motion, as if searching for a wallet or a pocket, but only stared out an uncovered window or a glance toward the wall and none of them even turned toward the young physician.

He left them four morphine tablets and told the wife how to give them by having her husband dissolve them under his tongue and to drink plenty of water, two or three quarts a day. She thanked him and he left the room. She called out of the door and thanked him again as he walked toward his horse.

About a week later, when coming back to his office after a long call, he found a cured ham and a croker sack full of cabbages on his doorstep. Dr. Brookshire kept three horses, which took a full time hostler caring for them and to keep one saddled, ready for the road day and night.

There were three other doctors in the town, two at the same time. Dr. Love was there, a short time earlier. Then, Dr. Holt and Dr. Speck came for several years while Dr. Brookshire practiced here. He had planned to stay only two or three years, but the two or three years turned into nearly sixty.

All of the doctors who came here had bought some farm land during their stay, probably at or near its peak in 1919. It seems, as always, it was exceedingly more desirable and productive when expensive and exorbitantly priced. But, when dirt cheap, near worthless, it could not be given away, even for the price of a few years back taxes.

During this time, the young doctor bought forty acres of good cotton ground. He got two tenants to live on it and sent to Murphreesboro, Tennessee, for a pair of twelve hundred dollar mules. When unloaded from a cattle car on a railroad side track, they drew a crowd like a three-ring circus. The massive, light chestnut, brown mules, nearly the size of draft horses, were thought to be the biggest, prettiest mules ever seen in the county. They were matched and said to work well together.

He bought the best gear Orgill Brothers, a wholesale hardware company in Memphis, was able to find, harnessing the pair like a Fifth Avenue coach team. The light, fawn colored mules, wrapped in heavy, dark, leather harness, studded with shining, rowed brass, from blinders to breeching, made a striking picture indeed, pulling a wheeled cultivator rapidly down cotton middles or a bright, new, orange Studebaker wagon to the gin, loaded with cotton. They made a much better showing, than any other field mules, plowing cotton in the Delta. He said they did a better job. They needed it.

Two years later, the bank sold them, along with the forty acres. The total amount not enough to pay the twelve hundred dollars for the mules, with nothing on the harness. Dr. Brookshire soon realized he was a doctor, not a cotton farmer. In later years, he would talk about his farming experience, with a laugh. But, it must have been a crushing blow at the time. He had plenty of company, however, and sometimes their crowd was increased by only the date of a summer rain.

The town grew slowly from its beginning. A railroad water tank, supplying water pumped from Hushpuckena Creek for the engines, was moved to Shelby. That stopped any further railroad development here. Shortly afterwards, an oil mill tried to locate here, but could buy no land to build on.

Joe Raggo's saloon, one of the first buildings here, was built on a high bluff of the creek bank just to the east of the railroad as it passed over the trestle. A wide walkway of heavy railroad timbers, with wide railings extended from the railroad embankment over to the saloon. Each day the schedules for two passenger trains, in each direction, allotted a twenty minute stopover at the saloon.

During the fall, three gins roared away daily, except Sundays, for almost four months, beginning in early August, pulling and snatching the vibrant, snowy fiber from its seed. White, steel bound, partially jute covered bales were moved out in railroad boxcars, as were the mounds of fuzz covered seed forked by hand to fill the same cars. The stretch was on in the fall, tugging and pushing hard. Cotton had to be gotten out of the field and to the gin, then moved to a spinner or later to a compress. The seed to a local oil mill. Everybody was busy. No time for wonder or thinking. The chase ongoing, only to run with the hounds. The toil and sweat and the struggle, squeezed the last hours from each day. The slow, regular, steady activity of winter's cold and heat of summer was ratcheted up to a high fervor.

Income for the entire year, their very existence, hung white in the field and had to be gathered, then moved to the gin, all in a few short weeks. But, with the first bales, came some money and time was taken on weekends to spend it. The stores hired additional clerks, were filled with new goods, all sent by train in July. Wares were placed on more attractive display. Innovative advertising and sales appeared. The town was full on weekends. Wagons of cotton arrived early Saturday morning, each with four or five smiling faces and lined up for half a mile from each gin. By noontime, there were three or four hundred people with seventy-five wagons and teams in the small town. Everybody had a little money to spend and were anxious to part with it. The tenants, having little all year except a livable, monthly furnish since March, were now ready to buy. To buy things before they got picked over. To have something to show, to put on the wagon and take home.

Occasionally he needed a new coat or new shoes for church, something that will impress his friends. But, he also needed a few other things, things to put on his table or hang by a nail on the wall, things he could put in a box or in a trunk and look at now and then, to take out and show a close friend, to have something to know about and to see, something that was his, to add to his accumulated goods. He would surrender his money for a suitcase or a trunk, shiny ebony black with polished brass edges and corners, to gather dust standing empty by a doorway. He may buy a bag of dyed feathers, red and blue and green, to hang on a nail or sit on his table. But, never a picture. He had no need for a picture. The rare photograph was different.

The grand prize of all, his most treasured possession, would be a chifforobe, with a door that locked and he would blame this purchase on his wife. A tall half drawered, half doored, heavily shellacked box, the door covered with a mirror, its backside covered with cardboard. The long mirror, wavy as ripples on a pond. It cost nineteen dollars and seventy-five cents and he would stand it up in his wagon to take home. Driving the mules with a far off, unconcerned look, as if he wasn't even aware of it, or was accustomed to carrying home treasure. For two months Momma's chifforobe was the topic of the children's and neighbor's conversation. Then, with that exhausted and no longer listened to, how "Momma lost the chifforobe key and what Daddy would do if she didn't find it."

Like all homosapiens, be he king or peasant, the old Commodores' descendants, a Rockefeller or a Mellon, he had to have his things, things with which to cover himself or take to his nest, things of value to show. A new coat and shoes for church, a shellacked chifforobe, with a long wavy mirror and a key.

A Delta tenants Conspicuous Consumption. Though Mr. T. Veblen, not here to label it such. Had he been, the essence of his treatise would have remained unchanged, only diverting somewhat its illusion.

Merchants, as always, had baited the trap. Kerosene and gas mantles glowed late Friday and Saturday nights, pulling the crowds like nocturnal insects and candle flies into the light, drawing all the cotton money they could attract. The town was alive Saturday afternoon and night. A moving swarm of bodies. From babies and children to old men and women. A mass, stacked with teams of mules, wagons, and flying and crawling insects. A grand horde of turmoil. The yearly outlet of the entire labor force. All swarming and in close motion, into the night, moving and talking and hollering and rubbing and sweating, held tight by the faint, yellow glow of store lights, compressed to a dense, straining bundle of moiling activity and bound fast, like iron filings to a magnet, held by a similar force, uncaring and unpalpable, but just as firm. And, like iron filings, as long as the force would last. Loud rolling voices from the crowd mumbled and incoherent. Voices everybody could hear but nobody understood, or wanted to understand, and nobody cared.

They were just there, each to announce his place with yells or grunts or screams or howls of laughter. Gold Crest 51 beer, right from the brewery in Memphis, green as alfalfa hay, added to the turmoil and bedlam.

Then, the wrong card would fall or a dice roll unbalanced or top heavy, the wrong word or a noticed touch, inappropriate and mis-served, a knife flashed or a pistol would pop. Loud screams, then quiet for ten minutes and the bluster and uproar would start again. The mass finally dispersing after midnight. The next Saturday there would be a troupe of gypsies with fortune tellers and horses and mules to trade and sell and steal. A minstrel the following Friday or Saturday night, the performers needing no charcoal or paint, but the tent filled to overflowing and shows until late. These weekends lasted through late October or mid November, then the cotton and the money were gone, half of an entire year's work dissipated on a few weekends, surviving a cold winter again on borrowed money.

A farmer with fifty houses full of tenants asked Old Man Thompson one morning what he thought about all this clowning and hollering and waste being carried on each Saturday night. The old man hesitated a moment, then while gazing off in the distance, he answered. "You know, I hear people carry on that same way in the big ballroom, atop the Waldorf Astoria, each Saturday night 'til three or four in the morning and those folks up there are dressed up, too, and drinking some of that good whiskey. But, they don't feel no better and it don't get 'em no drunker than this Gold Crest 51 beer. They say they come there with chauffeurs drivin' 'em, too. They got the same thing on the Peabody Roof in Memphis and all weekend at them country clubs up there. They tell me, there's a lotta them folks dodging their banker, too, don't want to see him. But, you take a tenant here, all of 'em. He's not worried 'bout nothing. He don't know what he owes and don't care. He ain't dodging nobody. If he wants something, he'll come look you in the eye and ask you for it and he'll get it, too. He knows you gonna take care of 'im and if something happens to 'im, he knows you gonna take care of his widow and chillun, long as they can hoe cotton. Why, he's got a better deal than that fella up there dancin' on top of the Peabody or the Waldorf and he knows it, too. That's probably what he's hollerin' and laughin' 'bout."

Old man Thompson spit across the store front and gazed again in the distance, he let up awhile and sort of caught his breath, then turned and asked. "What do you spend your money for, Mr. Scott?"

There it was for eighty years or more, in dozens of towns all over, from Memphis to Vicksburg, the resources of this Delta, its labor force, propelled by cotton. Like all creatures, from ants to man, their most efficient method of production and existence had organized and structured their society. Cotton production built this one.

Most of these towns are quiet now. Machines and chemicals in the fields, the tenants moved on and with them the conduit for some of the cotton money flowing to small town merchants. Without this flow, the merchants' business collapsed and they left. Their only resource gone, the well dry, their empty buildings having served their purpose, soon time ravaged and dilapidated, were swept away and the earth they blanketed, will again be put to the plow and maybe covered with cotton.

An area just to the east of the town was, at one time, a Choctaw Indian Camp, that probably lasted for hundreds of years. After a rain, in the freshly plowed field, flint arrowheads could easily be found along with pottery shards. The place has been labeled a "historic site." But, not enough of previous settlements has been searched for or found to prevent its partial destruction by highway construction. Three hundred yards to the west on a small knoll overlooking the bottom and Hushpuckena Creek, remnants of a mound exists. But, time has about erased the soft earthen structure. If future archeologists ever search, a campfire site may be found and dated. But, only a few shards of pottery and the flint chips will remain as evidence and a reminder of the hundreds of years of Indian habitation, then probably used only as a hunting camp. There will be much less of the hundred years the area spent as a local farming center. Only a few bricks related to nothing or maybe an iron ring or buckle from a mule bridle will lay buried to mark its existence. Though the farmer's iron will eventually dissolve with rust into the warm, moist earth, the Stone Age man's flint will not. It will remain longer than the marble in Athens, as sharp and precise as when he chipped it.

Uncle Bob took a long, deep breath and rested awhile. Then, before I could help him, he effortlessly reached and picked up a glass of water and drank. I had heard most of these stories before from Daddy and Uncle Bob, too, but it seemed now, he told them in more detail, as if he actually saw all of this again. He told them with an intensity, too, that I had never heard before, like he knew all this was about to fade away, but, being carved in someone's memory, it could last awhile yet. Like the poet said:

> "Yet, do not grieve;
> She cannot fade, though thou hast not thy bliss,
> Forever wilt thou love, and she be fair!
> Heard melodies are sweet, but those unheard
> are sweeter; therefore, ye soft pipes, play on."

∞

Across his yard, the store he saw, last housed a revival meeting, a place of seeking and comfort, of restoring belief, for some, renewal of hope, which sometimes was transformed into reality and knowing. The building now, only a collapsing brick shell of a structure, overgrown in the Delta foliage of rank weeds and masses of trumpet vines, absent any hope and belief and knowing, which had long since gone, with most if its mortal aspirants and like some of those left, awaiting its final breath, its extinction and doom into oblivion.

Store in Hushpuckena-Bolivar County Mississippi 1902

But, there it was. He saw it and the moving crowd, not an illusion or phantom of the oblivious, forgotten past, but real, immovable and unyielding as pride and honor, courage and belief, fixed in slow time, like caught on a silvered plate that haunts his memory, to know whether deities or mortals or both. That hot July night, almost sixty years ago, was as vivid and clear to him as it had been then. The wide, barred, glowing windows, the bright open space of the double doors, the gravel road filled with cars and people stirring about, their usual thunderous open air voices and laughter, subdued all waiting.

A crowd of eighty or ninety people clumped together on a gravel road, standing in front of an empty, abandoned Chinaman store, thinly clad for the late July afternoon. Some would be at five or six revivals during the summer and at their church on Sundays and Wednesday night. But, most would attend only this one revival and no more during the summer months. These were Thomas Jefferson's people. His crowd of Americans, his folks, his voters. All yeoman farmers or descendants of yeoman farmers and they had come again together, in search of an answer or reassurance of the answer they had found. They were waiting and standing around, shifting slightly, on the tiny stones, exchanging smiling faces and greetings. Not having seen one another during the past week, some were shaking hands, presenting a calm, relaxed composure, with talk of crops, cotton, and the weather. Always cotton and the weather, and now in July, of boll weevils. Then, there was this heat, flies and mosquitoes. But inside, fans were turning and pints of Black Flag fly spray had been blown into the air.

The Hushpuckena church was to have another revival, another reawakening and witnessing for the Lord, to store even more, in a far off home. A protracted meeting, not in a hillside brush arbor or towered cathedral, not even a simple chapel or meeting house, but in a window barred, Delta July hot, store building. To hear about sin, their sin, the old haunting phantoms of guilt and fear and the fiery wrath of God and his swift retribution. About Satan, his temptations, the temptations of the flesh, of Satan's hordes after each one of them. Then, of God's acquittal and his undeserved rewards, his merciful forgiveness, his redemption and salvation. The sweeping, recurrent narrative, complete, intact, unaltered and unabridged, the sum total of it all. Not in a steepled, spired auditorium with lofty belfried cupola, but in the white washed, homely, unadorned splendor of a hundred and fifty watt, light bulbed country Chinaman store. The brilliance of the bulbs shot through the barred windows beneath the tin covered porch, across seventy feet of gravel road onto a railroad, sidetrack platform, lined with black faces. They were soon covered in darkness and no sound to betray their presence, waiting for the young white preacher to show his strength, his calling by the Lord, to see if the tongue in his head could match the spirit in his bosom, to witness, if he had been called to preach or the plow.

The revival meeting was old in America when the constitution was adopted. From Europe it came to the eastern seaboard in the 1720s, or earlier, and followed the settlers westward. Baptists had taken it over in the 1850s and pushed it deep into the south, into every clearing and cabin and settlement. First along the rivers and streams and then overland, on horseback and on foot.

Irish Catholics, Kelly's, O'Malley's, and Riley's, the nearest priest in Natchez or New Orleans, had also attended revivals and were baptized after them and married because of them. The revivals, then Sunday preaching and prayer meetings and Sunday school had replaced the priest and he was now forgotten and alien and suspect, with his tight, stiff, rampart collar, his long black cassock, and dark Mediterranean face.

They preferred the individual religious experience, the heightened emotionalism, to the doctrine of any church, a God they could feel and see and shout about and laugh about and cry about, a God that would pull a man from the hell of a fiery lake and with his legions of angels, sword in hand, do battle with the hordes of Satan and with apocalyptic swiftness, slay the group en masse, and reign a thousand years on earth, over his born again righteous subjects. This, they could see and did see and know and feel, and had read to them and preached to them. There it was, black and white, chapter and verse, scripture, the Holy Writ, God's own word. They read it, they feared it, they saw it in a portrait, they not only would not, but could not, forget.

The rigorous doctrine, memorized prayers, those read from a book, recitations in Latin, all heresy. Too, the long robes, burning incense, a man forgiving sins, intercession, praying on beads, nothing but heathenism. Then, the genuflections to a statue, burning candles, worshipping Mary, prayers of intercession to Saints, the worst kind of blasphemous idolatry. All with a gowned and costumed Italian in Rome, Italy, wearing a two foot hat, the final arbiter. Certainly, this had to be, without a doubt, this was, if not, the antichrist, then surely paganism. This was alien, foreign, outlandish. It was undemocratic, not even American. Heresy, heathenism, blasphemy, and idolatry, even the antichrist and paganism, just what the preacher said the sword of God was against. They had been away too long. They would have no part of it. The revivals gave them what they wanted, what they needed, what they were missing. They continued, multiplied, spread, came to Hushpuckena in the whitewashed, hundred and fifty watt bulbed Chinaman store.

That hot, sultry, July, Monday night they were ready. Ninety strong. The store packed, ready for Satan, his temptations. He had gotten them all. All had sinned, all sinners. God's fiery wrath, his just retribution, and they knew his compassionate forgiveness and redemption.

Brother Barrett introduced Calvin and the young preacher was on his feet, Bible in hand, head held high, at the pulpit, almost before the older man could step aside. He never returned Brother Barrett's glance, but kept his gaze at the crowd as his Bible was firmly placed on the pulpit and he appeared to read from it, though he knew well, his text, by memory. He read it so as to concentrate on only the tone and cadence of his resonant, baritone voice. As he began, he read the Lord's Prayer to warm up, slowly and distinctly enunciating each word.

The deep, sonorous rhythm floated out over the audience and on past the railroad platform, where only widened white orbs shown in the dark night. Efforts of respiration and cicada the only other sounds. The crowd then was seated and he took off.

"In the beginning, on the sixth day God created this pristine, unseasoned, green, winterless conservatory, not just earth or water or life, yet all of each, together, inseparable, indivisible, fruits and berries, all manner of food illimitable, shame and suffering, anguish, fear and pain all alien. An Eden of serenity and pleasure, contentment and comfort. Into all this wonder and magnificence, he placed a man, his friend and his companion.

Out of the clay of the ground he formed him, and blew into his nostrils the breath of life and so man became a living mortal."

He looked down toward his Bible now and he began to read:

"God created man in his own image, in the divine image he created him. The Lord God settled him in the Garden of Eden and gave him this order. You are free to eat from any of the trees of the garden, except the Tree of Knowledge, of Good and Evil; from that tree you shall not eat. For the moment you do, you are doomed to die."

He paused a moment and went on:

"Then, the Lord said. It is not good for man to be alone. I will make a suitable partner for him. So, the Lord God cast a deep sleep on the man and while he was asleep he took out one of his ribs and closed up its place with flesh. The Lord God then built up into a woman the rib that he had taken from the man. When he brought her to the man, the man said, 'This one at last is the bone of my bone and flesh of my flesh. This one shall be called woman, for, out of her man, this one has been taken.' That is why a man leaves his father and mother and clings to his wife and the two of them become one body. The man and his wife were both naked and they felt no shame.

Man was in the glory of his day then and the pride of his strength. He feared no danger. He felt no sickness. He knew not of the groan or sigh at pain. He went forth fearlessly upon the face of the earth, his Eden.

What a piece of work was this man. How infinite in faculties! In form and moving how express and admirable! In action how like an angel! In apprehension how like a God! He gloried in the extent of his knowledge, in the vigor of his understanding and strove to search, even into what the Almighty had concealed."

Calvin had their attention now. All eyes were focused on him. They knew the story, but the melodious baritone floated out and brought it home once again. They had heard some genuine stem-winders talk on it before. Some true veritable water-ripplers preach it. But, Calvin was a local boy, one of their own, almost family, and this made the sweet revelation flow certain, authentic, and once more, as unvarnished gospel truth.

The deep, undulating resonance soared out through the open door and barred windows, out over the rough gravel road, and struck hard at the tier of immobile, hushed faces on the railroad platform. They had heard that white preachers didn't really preach, they just talked. But, this young white preacher was putting out something now. They knew he had been called. Why, he was even preaching from the Bible, was putting the Bible up there where you could see it.

Calvin labored on. "God had made man, his friend, his companion, made him in God's own image, placed him in a winterless Eden, given him a helpmate, a wife, made him free of want and need. Then, the crowning gift, the ultimate ability, the almost Godly power." And Calvin's voice lowered to a loud whisper when he said this, "God had given man the opportunity of choosing, an unrestrained, unfettered free will. No rein was placed on him. He could achieve or contrive as he saw fit. He could choose to follow God's divine law or he could manage his own. While in his boundless, bountiful Eden, only a solitary restraint was placed on him. Last, as a supreme act of mercy and compassion, God had given him hope. He knew he would need it.

But, God had brought into being a different creature, an experiment, a test even of his own prowess, a study, yet of his very skill and competence. A changed cerebral cortex, a new neuronal pattern, a neo-pallium. Yes, a novel, recent, even untried, six layered cortex. He created, verily fabricated him, an immortal human being, a creature that stood erect, upright. One to straighten his shoulders, stand his tallness, and defiantly, with insolence if he chose, brazenly look him straight in the eye. He had given him a choice, a free will. God's own experiment to achieve a companion. A companion, though, with all his endowed virtue to choose Him or one to defy His presence, His very existence.

God now had a friend, a companion, and to further show His love of this man. He had placed him in a perpetual Eden, a place of plenty, free of fear and anguish, free from toil and want, a place of warmth and love and the brightness of eternal life. With all of this, there remained the one restriction, he must never think himself a God, he must never eat of the Tree of Knowledge, his eyes must not be opened as those of a God, he must not know all that God knows, he must not know of good and evil, he must never know shame."

Calvin hesitated a moment as he seemed to look squarely at each one of them. Then, he slowly pressed on, again in that soft audible whisper. "God so loved man, He gave him a free will, He let him decide for himself. Now he must chart his own path, divine the right course. His well ordered domain and his map were gone. He had to bear the burden of freedom of choice. There was no direction, no authority, no guide to plot the maze, only freedom of choice. His tranquil mind soon changed."

Calvin looked toward the open door, then with a raised brow, and just short of a grin, he added. "Man probably needed two or three more layers of cortex, but he could only go with what he had. Man's six layered cortex became restless. He was not appeased by all he had. He began to dream, to brood and ponder. He thought of nothing else, why could not he think as a God, know as a God? A violent storm arose in his consciousness. Impulse after turbulent impulse shot through his cortex—wave after heightened wave followed. The cortex began to ripple and roil, then undulate and billow as it seethed in discontent. Darkness came. Night fell across the cortex. Lightning cracked and flashed. He was in turmoil and confusion. The storm surged on. Why had God placed the tree so near, such beauty and desire at the very center of the garden, while he was all around it, then deny him; he must never touch it? What else was there to know? Why could he not be as a God? He was made in the image of God. This worried him. He thought on it for days, just one tree in the entire garden. Why not have it all?"

Then, Calvin's voice seemed to quicken as he went on. "The serpent came, then the woman. Surely she would not betray him. God had placed it all there for him. Certainly, he meant for him to enjoy it. Then, she forced his hand, it was taken, he ate the fruit. His eyes opened, he saw his nakedness, he was ashamed.

In the evening of the day, the breezy time shortly before sunset, God came into the garden. The man and his wife hid themselves among the trees and covered themselves with leaves, for they were afraid. Afraid because they were naked. And they told God this. Then, He knew they had eaten from the tree of which He had forbidden them.

When asked, the man blamed it on the woman, whom God had put there with him. She then blamed it on the serpent who tricked her into eating it. Each placing the fault somewhere else. God knew better and because of their sin, our first parents' eternal sin, a sin to carry through all the ages, a sin of greed and disobedience, they were banished from the garden. Cast out of Eden forever.

She will bear the intense pangs of childbearing. 'In pain, you will bring forth children.' To the man he said," and Calvin began a slow crescendo, "Cursed be the ground before you! In toil shall you eat its yield all the days of your life. Thorns and thistles shall it bring forth to you as you eat of the plants of the field. By the sweat of your face shall you get bread to eat, until you return to the ground from which you were taken. For you are dirt, and to dirt you shall return."

Calvin's loud, high pitch abruptly faded as he slowly cast his glance toward the floor. Bill Rogers twisted in his chair. George Smite looked down slowly, stroking his bald head. Joe Harold gazed at the ceiling. Several of the women just slowly shook their heads.

From across the gravel on the platform, a loud voice came. "Yeah, he did it, he mighty well sho' did it, he et dat fruit, offin' dat tree, dat the Lord tol' him don't bother. Then, the Lord put 'im out, put 'im outta dat garden. Lord knows he did it." A loud solitary hand clap, then again silence across the road.

Calvin lifted his gaze from the floor as the mellow baritone flowed again, an unrecoiling wave, spreading across the gathering once more. "And we all here, all of us, are burdened with the sin of Adam, our earthly father, our progenitor, who bequeathed to us, to all generations to come after him, his eternal transgression, his perpetual sacrilege, his wickedness, corruption and immorality, the temptation to submit to greed and disobedience. The siren's song seduced him, the enticement and allurement of the transient, ephemeral gratifications and pleasures of this world."

He went on to enumerate some of the transient pleasures they all had succumbed to. He went through a litany of faults, impurities and iniquities. Then, he came to strong drink, spirituous hard liquor—ALCOHOL. This had been his most grievous sin, his worst transgression. He told them he had fought it for five years. This was the most grievous because it would lead to all others and they all had been touched by it and felt it. They had seen it in themselves or in their homes or neighbor's home. It was Satan's own weapon—ALCOHOL—and he came down hard on this word. Put here by him, by Satan, to torment man, to trap his innocent victims and, were it not for the grace of God, he would use it to enslave the entire planet.

Calvin went on to say Satan had used it to "entrap him, to

subjugate him, to crush him in his powerful hellish grasp, and for five years he held him there in servitude and bondage, tyrannized by and shackled to alcohol. A prisoner in an iron, doorless cage, with bolted walls that moved in closer and tighter upon him each day, more limiting and confining with each sunrise, then after the sun the phantom, permeable, howling walls, twisting and grinding, turning and crushing with each stone hard, rock encrusted and toothed, masked face, bat winging toward him, through the blackened, lightless space, unending until they dissolved again in the eastern light which showed the walls closer and tighter upon him yet. No way to escape, no light to see, all hope abandoned, surrendered to Satan, possessed by Satan, free will, the notion of choice, all abdicated, to endure apart, in solitude, in a desert alone, secluded, in hopeless despair." Calvin painted a terrible picture. He awoke in the middle of the night, he said, crying for liquor. He would walk the streets trying to find it, had even stolen to buy it. He had nearly lost his wife and children, had almost starved. There was no immunity to it, the demon possessed him, possessed his will and his mind. He was lost, he was seized by Satan and could not comprehend it. In his inevitable despair, in his intractable loneliness, there was but a single alternative-prayer. He prayed to the Lord, he prayed hard on his knees, he cried. Then, by the goodness of God, by the power of his grace, God had released him, had released Satan's hold on him. He had set him free.

 Calvin was on his knees now, to the front of the pulpit, his voice rising, hands clasped together outward toward the ceiling. Through the grace of God, by his infinite mercy and forgiveness, he was freed, freed from Satan, freed from sin. He was saved. They all can saved. Each one here can be saved. By the grace of God they would be saved. Repent now for your sins. Pray, ask forgiveness, and you shall be saved.

 Calvin was in a hard, rolling sweat, he had them. They were seized by him, in his grip. The crowd had been still, immobile, almost transfixed in their chairs, motionless and inert, without compulsion to move and like a vibrant wind against sails his words had seized them. Some were on the edge of their seats, white, stilled eyes aglare, fastened on him, mouth breathing, almost mesmerized. Several turned a furtive, stealthy glimpse toward the door, quick and dry mouthed, almost as if they expected to see Satan, fork in hand, eyes ablaze, standing there, then move into the room.

Still on his knees as he slowly again lowered his head and held his clasped hands to his chest, he remained there silent for a moment, then rose up and went to the pulpit, got his Bible and slowly walked toward the open door.

As he moved down the narrow aisle, sweat still clinging to his brow, there was a peaceful, calm expression, about his face. Not a haughty, vain arrogance, but almost a relaxed smile of accomplishment and winning. Some later even said it looked like a smile of redemption. All of the audience turned and gazed at him as he walked through the crowd. Some in whose eyes burned an indomitable longing and yearning and the last desperation of hope, some with an amazed, distant vision staring above or to the front of him, their stone, immobile faces vacant and bland in wonder and bewildering awe, their eyes holding a faint, star-like glimmer in anticipation of the arrival of optimism and belief.

The young preacher had done well. They were pleased and proud. Calvin turned to neither side as he strode toward the darkened opening, but with his side vision he saw an old friend, Roy Shannon, seated on the back row. Roy must have come in after he started preaching. His eyes, though, never shifted. Still, his gaze became more intent, not in ecstasy but vigorously determined and engrossed in satisfaction and peaceful content, his vision fixed to the distance across the platform, somewhere out in the July laden darkness, the serene redeeming stillness of the night. He departed through the opened door. The crowd followed. The first night's revival had ended.

Calvin stood at the door as the crowd walked out. A few who had to pass close by shook his hand, but kept a downward gaze, never looking up at him. Only several older men shook his hand and met his eye with a smile and thanked him for such powerful preaching. Most, though, got out without looking toward him and had a strange, drawn expression on their face, a look as if they had been discovered or surprised in a suspicious or compromising situation. A strained, downward glance, as if Calvin had seen back behind that drawn expression to the cause of their feelings of guilt and fear. A place they thought belonged only to themselves, remote, hidden, and isolated, locked away in that secluded simian, bestial part he had opened and written across their face. Calvin was too young to know all of this, but he had told each one of them about their own concealed sins, their veiled errors, and their cloaked backsliding, of the facades, the defenses and the masks they erected and put on to cover and disguise all of this. As soon as they passed him, though, this was mercifully forgotten. Their iniquities all wiped from the slate, only their minor infractions and the good they had done, left in their memory, the relaxed, peaceful composure returned.

Roy was the last one out of the building. He had just been sitting there, seemingly benumbed and dazzled. He had known Calvin for several years. They had been on some outings together in the past. But, this was different now. Calvin was a changed man, he could readily see it. As he passed Calvin, there was a firm handshake and a smile, but nothing suggesting a hug or embrace of any kind, just two old friends meeting again, in a crowd and slowly passing by.

The following nights Roy was there, not on a back row but toward the front of the building. The crowds were getting a little bigger each night in spite of the heat and the swarming giant candle flies, the Black Flag failed to immobilize, and each night he hit hard again at their sins and wrong doings. It seemed at times, even, that he was preaching to a group of convicts, his words were so hard, and the mellow baritone would rise with force, to a booming crescendo each time he told of liquor and of Paul's powerful message, "Human beings live at the center of a cosmic drama, that reaches to the core of each one of us, as the forces of good and evil battle within the individual." Then, he always offered them hope. Belief-Belief will save us, belief not from the intellect with a shallow, depthless reason, but from the heart. Sustained, undaunted, unyielding belief, from the old infallible axioms of the heart.

Calvin had never gotten to Thomas Aquinas. He must have stopped with Augustine. Each night as the week wore on and he stood at the door after his long sermon, more of the attendants, as they came by, would look at him, squarely in the eye, when they shook his hand and thanked him.

After the second night, Roy even stood there a short time bantering with his old friend and the last two or three people to leave the building. Each night they talked a little longer, but always about the sermon.

The last night, toward the end of the sermon, Calvin was on his knees again, hands clasped across his chest, praying, his soft mellow voice easily spreading out over the attentive group. Every eye was on him, hearing each word, as he thanked the Almighty for the bounty bestowed on all of them and asked for forgiveness for their numberless sins. Then, after a short pause, he again bowed his head and asked the Lord to grant each one of them the knowledge and the wisdom to know and to understand His will and the faith and the courage to carry it out. He kept his head lowered another moment, then slowly stood up and walked back to the pulpit, but he stood in front of it this time with his Bible held across his chest.

"Yes," he said in a soft voice, "there is tragedy here. That's our lives. Our lives are full of it. Tragedy and travail. Born with the burden of consciousness, the price of which is a sentence of death. Searching for a difficult, sometimes hidden, truth, you cannot find while looking so hard, then when relaxing a bit, it may be found along with the comedy there, added by fools and buffoons and actors passing as fools and buffoons. But, there is hope, eternal hope, and it is here," and he held his Bible up high. "We have been saved from all of this, saved if we will but believe."

Again, he looked out over the crowd and slowly let his hands fall to his sides, holding his Bible in one of them. Then, the mellow distinct voice continued, "We don't need emperors and bishops, theologians and councils to chart our path to it, our path to the truth. We have it all right here." And, he held his Bible up high, straight up over his head, then out toward the crowd as he repeatedly said, "We have it all here, here in this book. With help, we can will ourselves to it."

He slowly walked a short ways down the aisle, then stood still as he turned to each side with his Bible still held high and he began shaking it as he repeatedly said, "It is all here. Here in this book." Shaking, as if trying to shake the truth out of it, out of his Bible onto the crowd. He again drew the Bible toward his chest and held it there with his head slightly bowed, his eyes in a downward gaze. He took a few steps toward the door, then stopped and, still holding his Bible tightly to his chest, he turned around and looked back again toward his empty pulpit, where he had stood each night, for five consecutive nights, where he had stood and knelt and preached and prayed until he was wet in the July heat of the store, and where he had felt an uplifting unlike anything he had ever experienced, but similar, he remembered, to that while lying in his bed as a child. Where he had seen the look of renewed hope and determination and perseverance and maybe even belief in some faces, put there by his preaching and his work and his sweat.

As he stood there amidst the crowd, he felt almost transcended, as he did the other four nights, transcended beyond this mortal world of heartbeat and breathing, of sweat and sin. He wanted to stay there longer. It seemed he had searched for this all of his life. But, a few seconds were all he had, as he could feel he already had lost some of the crowd. He knew it had been for them and they were staring at him. He slowly turned again and trudged toward the door. His eyes not cast off in the distant July night, but downward in the direction of the floor. The floor of a once busy, now abandoned Chinaman store. On to the door and he stood there and smiled and he shook hands with each one of them, while they left and thanked him again for his powerful message. Calvin was proud of what he had done, but he soon remembered that pride too, may not be good and he tried to reclaim the feeling he had, before he left the store. But that, too, was gone.

Again, Roy was the last to leave and they chatted awhile before Roy asked for a ride. They turned off the lights, locked the door, got in Calvin's car and left for the two and a half mile drive home.

As they drove home, there was little talk initially, except Roy telling him how well he had done. Calvin thanked him, but had little to say until Roy told him, "You know, Cal, with that ability you got you ought to think about running for office and gettin' into politics." Calvin didn't answer him right away, but after a short while he did. "Yeah, I been thinkin' about that some, but that's so treacherous and nothing is deader than a defeated politician. You never know what people might do 'cause they can change so quick. They will ride you on top of the waves one time, then some little somethin' come along, anything, and they'll sink you to the bottom and forget about ya the next. I'd rather get into somethin' more stable." After awhile he added, "I been thinkin' about farmin' again. Daddy's got that three hundred and twenty he's renting out. He might let me try it again. You know, I been reading about these soybeans they startin' to grow here. They say they've been makin' money on 'em up north, a lotta money for a long time." "Yeah, I been readin' about soybeans, too," Roy quickly added, "And some of 'em around here are tryin' 'em and doin' pretty good. We got some good varieties, too." "Yeah, they got to be good," Calvin said. "They're named after Confederate generals. They say that big Lee bean could make a man rich. I remember readin' not too long ago, that old man Henry Ford, at one time, had a bunch of chemists tryin' to make rubber outa soybeans. I never did find out what come of it, but if they ever do make rubber out of 'em we'll be ridin' on soybeans and they'll go sky high."

As they drove on through the night, they talked about growing soybeans, nothing but soybeans, about how many bushels they could make to the acre and the number kept increasing as they drove. They figured the price they could sell them for, the cost of growing them, how much they would make, the entire advanced science of soybean production and marketing. They even decided they might cut expenses by farming together, using the same equipment. They would only have to work six or seven months a year. Could spend all the time they wanted hunting and could fish some. Calvin might even want to preach some more, since he had gotten good at it, and might even run for office.

They should have gotten home in less than ten minutes, but they had been driving for more than an hour and a half before Calvin finally parked the car. When they got out, they were still planning and working out their strategy for the soybean project.

The next morning about nine thirty, Calvin's wife got a telephone call. She had been awake all night calling everybody she knew and some of her neighbors were with her. The deputy told her he had found Calvin and Roy in a bar over at Benoit, both passed out on the floor. He wanted her to come over and bring somebody to drive their car home. "I'll see that they stay at Toby's bar 'til you get here," he said. "Toby wants you to come on now and pick 'em up 'cause he's gotta close his place and lock up, and they ain't in no shape to drive.

There's a whole tablet full of figgers here," the deputy continued, "looks like somethin' they was workin' on. You can't read nothing but the first few pages, though. The table's covered with pencil shavin's, too. Musta used up two or three good pencils, with all this figgerin'. Toby said they'd been here drinkin' and talkin' and figgerin' all night. He never did know what they wuz figgerin' on, though. He said he thought one while they musta been figgerin' to make one'a them 'tomic bombs with all the figgerin' they wuz doin'." Calvin's wife had not said a word and the deputy never ceased. "I don't reckon they broke no laws, so I'll leave 'em here with Toby if you'll come on pick 'em up. Toby's got their keys and he said he'll keep the tablet for ya."

THE FOREST OF THE NIGHT

The Town Crier's Tale

Tiger, Tiger, burning bright
In the forest of the night;
What immortal hand or eye,
Could frame thy fearful symmetry?

William Blake
The Tiger

He was up early that morning. The big dipper still hung bright and full in the north sky. The radiator of his 1932 Chevrolet truck had long been hot and he turned the headlights off when the sun shown red in the east. He was driving alone. His 12-year-old would sleep for another hour. He usually went with him, but this time it was too early and, besides, the boy had hogs and chickens to feed. Two or three days each week he made these trips, touring the countryside in that Chevrolet truck buying scrap iron or any metal from tenants and farm headquarters alike.

It was lay by time now, mid July. They had already gotten their last furnish for the year and there would be no more money until cotton picking started the end of August, another six weeks. Iron ought to be coming in better, he thought. War had started a year and a half before that early July morning and scrap iron was going up almost weekly, now at fifty cents a hundred. Japan had been buying all they could get for ten years before that December 7, bringing the price from ten cents. It was still rising. Some had heard it was worth seventy cents a hundred in Memphis. The truck was moving well, had been since he started. It was hot and the engine purred. Hard, packed, clay gravel, smooth and level, covered the road. The old truck moving easily along, flowing across its surface. A tenant house sat by the roadside each quarter mile or so and he passed the near one with only a quick glance.

There was a feeble yellow light, faint and hardly visible in some windows when he passed and occasionally he could see cooking smoke slowly rising from the chimneys. The gray smoke slowly climbing straight up in the cool early July morning. Some houses were scattered out in the fields and a narrow two lane dirt road left the gravel and wandered off in their direction. Since the Civil War, the tenant cabin housed the labor force for the cotton fields. Slave quarters served the same purpose before that time. A mule barn sheltered the remainder of the work force for the fields. Instead of a yard or lawn, wrapped around most of the two or three room, metal roofed, frame structures, narrow strips of well swept, bare earth coiled close and hard like metal bands about a wooden box. Cotton rows pushed up to the very edge of these slender constraining aisles.

Surrounding those next to the road, cotton surged up close on three sides, out in the fields on all four. With only two steps from his back door or front porch, the tenant would be either in the cotton field or on the road. Saturday afternoons he was fleet of foot, when off the front porch onto the road and to town to get beered up with his friends or in a crap game to gamble away a week's wages or meet a girlfriend. On Sundays, when older, walking to church or on a winter night to follow dogs, towards the woods, on a coon hunt. Leaving the other door to the cotton field, his stride would be much slower. Carrying a hoe, his steps were more deliberate and contemplative as he studied the expanse of the field and the condition of each row, meditating on each weed or patch of grass he passed as if knowing he must remove it if he is to keep his house. But, he just might be able to put this off, wait until next time.

A few steps out back of the same house stood a three foot square cubicle, hardly head high, the open side of it partially covered by a misfitted, short croker sack, worn and translucent. The ground about the back door of the house without this accommodation was kept wet and covered with swarms of green fly, surfaced slime. A pitcher water pump stood a few yards away. Some front porches, the only one on the house, were covered with vines to shade the afternoon sitters from the summer sun. Always a mirror or some reflecting surface a foot or so square was nailed to a wall on the porch, put there to brighten an image that could hardly be seen in the darkness of a small room in the house. It reflected the results of a Saturday morning hair straightening or guided a razor before going to town. Some houses were surrounded by trees and well shaded. Occasionally a paling fence enclosed them along with a garden and fruit trees. Many had a small eight foot high deleafed tree, stuck in the front yard, limbs partially amputated, with a snuff bottle stuck on each short limb stub, almost covering the small tree. Strips of rags, blue and red, yellow and orange, hung on each limb, always placed just to the right and close by the front door steps, there to catch and hold anything that should not enter the house.

The sun now would soon be yellow in the east and was at his back as he rolled on faster toward the big highway. Passing close by two churches, he could see two others far back in the fields. The New Macedonia church sat high on a ridge banking Hushpuckena Creek. It had been there eighty-five years. Mount Evergreen on a mile or so to the west along the road was at the edge of a cotton field. It had a bell, as they all did, but unlike New Macedonia's bell, which stood enclosed in a tower at the point of the roof, it had no tower to lift it up and to rest within, but sat straddling two logs at the front of the church.

Thirty to thirty-five feet long and one-half as wide, the churches were usually full on their pastoral Sundays, two or three Sundays each month. Searing hot in the sweating summer with only a newspaper fan to combat the heat and swarming insects. The occasional palmetto, though, was a front seat prize, for the three hours from 11 o'clock to 2 o'clock and the few there were always moving in a wide displaying arc, somehow suppressing any evidence of sweating by its holder, who projected a countenance of cool composure and calm control, effortlessly clinging to each sound from the preacher's throat, never having to stop the fan to handkerchief her face.

The bone chill of deep winter was another time for displaying and show. Like a peacock in a strut it was the new bright colors of a coat or hat that always ventured to a front seat. With new loud clanking jewelry or new shoes that squeaked, a woman or man found it difficult to find a suitable place to sit. They would be up walking about through the small building, back to front and back again announcing their new shoes or ornaments, trying several seats, all of the same hard cypress boards, before a comfortable one was found.

When he turned north on No. 1 there was still no traffic

and he could see for a mile up the highway. Occasionally a thin blue fog hung over a slough or low place in the highway, but now the road was mostly straight and he could let the old truck roll.

He was going up toward Lewis' swamp. He had not been up there all year. By now, the Stanford boys would have some iron.

The settlement at Lewis' swamp was old. Some said it had been there long before the Civil War, since before the time of the Indian treaty. Back a ways from Australia Landing which was on the river, it had survived that settlement's fate, now claimed by the churning, roving currents. Most of the buildings there were made of cypress logs, some with boards added around a window or up next to the roof or an added side room made of boards, on cypress blocks. The sawmill had been put up there early and the age of the building could be told by its walls. Hand rived shingles covered most of the roofs. The only store there, though, had sheet metal veneer overlaying its once cypressed canopy.

Bo Wiggington owned the store and had been there thirty years. His father built it twenty years before Bo owned it, when he left Australia Landing just ahead of its collapse into the river. There were two other stores, or trading posts, there then, just to the south of the swamp. One since forty years before, started to trade with trappers and hunters coming out of the two hundred square mile swamp, dry only three months each year. The swamp then was thick with cane and briar, giant cypress and gum, oak and hickory and pecan and still abound with game. Some said the settlement had been a camp site, Major Fontaine had used when he surveyed the Delta swamp country after the Indian treaties.

Just to the north of the settlement, Hushpuckena Creek came out of the swamp and wound east, twisting and turning in its coiling, convoluted path, meanderous and writhing until it finally found the Sunflower forty miles away. On these dark waters the store owners and traders took their hides and furs, mink and raccoon, deer, and on occasion black bear, down to the

Sunflower and the Yazoo on to Vicksburg and on south, further, bringing back store goods and supplies on a steamboat.

He had lived at the swamp settlement, grown up there. He knew every family there. He knew their secrets. He knew every man, woman and child by their first name. His family had moved to the settlement when he was nine years old. He was living then in the hills in Tallahatchie County, the year the boll weevil had gotten there in its full fury, devastating the cotton. They left nothing in the fields, less than ten bales ginned in the entire county. The pest had come across from Georgia. Some had said they came from the sea islands and others said they came there from Mexico, in dolls stuffed with cotton seeds. Whatever their route, they were there, from the east, out of Georgia and cotton in most of the hill counties was destroyed. With no cotton, they had no money and no seed for the next year. People had to leave. His father followed an uncle who had fled the red clay hills ten to fifteen years earlier and moved to the swamp settlement.

The Stanford boys' grandfather, with several other ex-slave families, had come to the settlement shortly after the war. Now, the Stanford's were the only slave descendants left. The other land, back early was farmed in small patches of corn and cotton, by descendants of hill people and river fishermen and trappers and the original "river rats" who had acquired the land with Winchester's and by squatter's rights. The Stanford boys were different. They had stayed. They could read a map and a deed. They knew their property lines, which they never tried to move, nor did anyone else.

In a short time he was at Isaiah Stanford's, a log house, barn, corn crib, and several other buildings. Isaiah knew what he wanted and with little conversation he took him to the pile of iron, a mass jumbled up, heaped into a low flat mound.

There lay the old used iron, now worthless in farming, its time spent helping Isaiah wrench a living from the dark layered earth. Old worn or broken plow tools, a pitcher pump and pipe with a driving point, whose fine mesh brass strainer long since worn away by the deep sands, holding water, filtered across from the river, iron wheels, with the gear box from a mowing machine, built in a factory owned by Cyrus McCormick, plow points, part of a motor from a Model T Ford. Quite a stack of iron.

When he saw the iron lying there, partially covered with weeds, he did not walk toward it or approach it directly or straight on, but he stopped instantly in mid stride. Frozen and immobile, stalled, not moving, as if paralyzed, his head partially turned toward the iron, his eyes fixed on it, he hunkered down, like a good setter at the first scent of a quail, every muscle taut and strained, rigid and stiff without movement. As he then crept slowly past the iron in his low crouched stance, he turned to circle it, his head motionless, still partially turned toward the aged, worn metal, his eyes fixed in a hard, fierce, penetrating stare, like a predator circling his prey. He seemed to be trying to creep past the iron, without being seen or noticed by it, to sneak past it, to steal its secret. Seeing every piece of iron in the pile, he knew its value as well as the total of the stack. Every sense in his body was focused on the iron and he could feel it, he could feel the iron as he saw it, it was a part of him like his heartbeat and his breathing, which seemed to have stopped. He knew to the penny what it would bring. Before he stopped, his head slowly turned through a small arc, his vision still set on the iron, eyes doll like, as if a machine, scanning deep within the pile. As he finished circling the pile, he gradually lost his crouched stance and he began to thaw. His breath came easier and he moved the cigar stub to the side of his mouth. The muscles of his face were slackened, his expression began to relax a little and his beady eyes slowly crinkled as he looked up at Isaiah.

Isaiah had not moved either, but stood quiet and stork like watching him circle the iron pile. He was almost transfixed himself, totally absorbed and engrossed in what he saw. Isaiah never saw a man look at something like that before. He had bought a few cows and hogs over the years and he had seen other men buy them, many times, but he had never seen a man look at anything like this. He did not feel good about it either.

"Well, Isaiah, you got a nice little pile of iron here, about three hundred pounds I'd say." "Well suh," Isaiah answered, "I believe there's a little more than that, ain't it? Looks like to me there oughta be way over five hundred there on the ground."

Isaiah and the white man haggled lightly about the weight. Some of the haggling in easy jest, but with some harder shoves pretending jests. There was a line, though, that neither crossed. Never in the middle, but each knew where it was, knew how close he could get to it and he knew how hard he could push. A line invisible as breath, though impenetrable and solid, hard as iron, but sometimes wandering and broad as the river itself and like the river it was always there.

Both knew the iron was worthless where it lay, lying there dissolving into rust. It had to be moved to have any value and this man was Isaiah's only chance to move it. He had no way to take it to Clarksdale.

This had been Isaiah's fate, a farmer's fate, his father's and grandfather's alike. They had always sold into a buyer's market and bought from a seller's. They worked on their farm and in the fields all year. Then, one pay day, they sold their harvest for whatever they could get. The work of an entire year. Year after year they took their cotton samples to a buyer on the street and had to take whatever he offered or walk down the street to another office where they might be offered an eighth of a cent a pound more, but the buyer would short the weight more than enough to make up for it. They took what they were offered or took the cotton back home to rot.

With the iron trade, he felt better. Not completely helpless, he could bargain awhile. He did not feel run over, but he was against a congenital haggler, a trafficker and a marketer, a supreme exchange agent, and after watching that walk he wasn't so sure. With a few more offers and counters, the weight was decided at three hundred and fifty pounds and a dollar and a nickel changed hands.

Then, back on the big highway and more iron piles and more circling and smiles and smooth haggling and bargains struck. Though seemingly one sided and heavily weighted, this brought some value to the rusting iron lying there worthless. It was moved into trade and exchanged for money. Another cottage industry helping survival.

The truck's lights had been bright, three hours in the mid July night when he arrived at home and it had to strain mightily and grind hard to cross the railroad embankment, fifty yards from where he lived. With two and a half tons of iron, some copper pipes, several old radiators, and some worthless car batteries, he would soon be ready for a trip to Clarksdale.

When he came to the Delta in 1911, a nine-year-old, his family moved in with an uncle at the swamp settlement. They left the southeastern part of Tallahatchie County, the steep, red clay hilly part where, in just three years, the boll weevil took everything they owned. They did not give up much, though, only a meager subsistence.

The hills were old and furrowed when the weevil came, worn and used up like the people living there, mining and taking from the soil all the red clay would relinquish. Maybe the clay had called in the weevil pests just to get some relief and rest from the farmers who had looted and pillaged the last bit of sustenance from the hills. The inhabitants, too, were exhausted and spent, the red clay plundering and grasping more than it would surrender. Taking, like all dirt, the red earth greedy and ravenous taking still more, taking even beyond their will to endure.

Since that Yankee Whitney, had learned to make a cotton gin, by watching a cat pull feathers from a chicken through a wire fence, more than a century before, every blacksmith in the south had made one and they spread cotton across Georgia and Alabama, then filtered it into the hills of Mississippi. With the hungry cotton, they quarried and dredged the land more and more each year. Then continuing, they gouged it out, bleeding the raw, dull earth, leaving it barren and lifeless. The tarnished russet earth, unrevived and pumiced, had given all it could and it started dispossessing them and reclaiming its wealth. The soil's tearing from them continued, unrelenting and ruthless, leaving barefoot children with hollow, deep set eyes, their sallow faces drawn and narrow under greasy, straw hair, wresting away their last desire and hope. Their strength and will gone, their youth wrenched away, after their early twenties, still adhered and annealed to the land, the hill tenants resembled it, were a part of it, exhausted and desperate, despairing. The weevil seen as a scourge was only the last badger, goading them from this morbid, sterile, rust red earth.

The boy was called Clarence Wilbanks and he remembered leaving the hills, then the long trek through the Delta. Following their uncle there, they had heard the flat, alluvial Delta would be a refuge for them, a virtual sanctuary, an assured, protected place against the near starvation and misery afflicted on them by those barren, hungry hills where knee high, August cotton, without a square, bloom or a boll, across the entire field, to sucker or leach it, was green as a field of "nit-a-sodaed" (corn). With all the fruit of the cotton plant punctured or destroyed, the weevil swarmed on the food crops, ravishing beans and peas and all the pod-producing plants. Without legumes, ten bushel corn would be a hard survival.

His father of less than average height was withered and gaunt, wasted and thin. The old man's raw boned, cadaverous face covered with lined parchment like skin was scorched and drawn, desiccated by years in the sun-drenched, blustery cotton fields in the red, clay hill country. His beady, little eyes hollow, set deep and cloudy in their darkened, cavernous pits seemed fixed and robot like so when scanning a cotton field or rabbit thicket he slowly rotated his head through an arc, almost a half circle, his dark eyes motionless. Those fixed, piercing eyes had saved him though, probably more than once while engaged in one of the two entrepreneurial activities his slow brain had ever managed to contrive. Whiskey making.

While running off a batch several years before, he saw some revenuers as the horses topped a hill, almost half a county away.

He thought their horses' strides were different from any he had seen locally. He left the still, already fired and running, never returning and watched from a mile away, back in his dog trot shack, the same one his father was born in. He watched as they hid there for several weeks, waiting his return. The still collapsed in rust, overgrown in vines and saplings, except for the burnished copper coil carried off by one of his neighbors.

Leaving Tallahatchie county, the only move his father ever made that his neighbors said showed any "sense a'tal," was probably initiated by his stomach rather than his brain. His other single attempt at the entrepreneur's art involved that of an occasional hog theft. But, living in an area of experts, he had been threatened and warned before of this, more than once and his successes were transient and rare. This endeavor, however, was more instinct than higher cerebral activity and he had long ago left this practice to those with a quicker reflex and a more honed edge. Learning was difficult for the old man. It always had been. Never seeming to apply the results of previous attempts, he was constantly chafed by the same old grit, writhing from the same old inscrutable, illimitable pumice that had always abraded and excoriated his consanguineous forebears, whose lineage probably reached back to the Celts.

His ventures were more a reaction or recoil than planned deliberate undertakings, always acting with rashness and rapidity, as if pushed by superstition or fear or some primitive visceral need. The urge to leave Tallahatchie County had struck him one morning early, late in August while he sat near his porch, back in the dog trot, drinking boiled coffee, from the same stone mug his grandfather had drunk from. His eyes were fixed on the haze, the thin blue vapor lying like a fog or smoke over a distant thicket down in the cool of the creek bottom and by noon his wagon was slowly creaking toward the west, two rabbit mules and his family, on the only road he knew in that direction.

He sat there with his wife on a board, a hand sawed plank, across the front of the wagon, jolting over the brick hard, rough clay. Three children behind them, wide eyed and anxious, on a thick cushion of grass hay, hurled up and down with each solid contact of the iron rims on the stony, August fired earth. The little stunted mules weighted down by the oversized collars and hames around their neck, trudging on, hesitant, uncertain and slow, sometimes stumbling as they groped along, stepping on their shadows under the hard, fierce mid summer sun. The old man's eyes fixed on a mirage, toward the west, a distant image he had never seen. "That Delta, where they grows shoulder high cotton, all the way from Memphis to Vicksburg." The only other idea or vision evoked in his vacuous brain, "Hit's distaway." That was all he needed. His hard, jerky tough body, though, was well adapted and conditioned to respond to the slow fury of his short circuited guidance system, evolved for only cunning and survival.

The wagon slowly rolled on over the rough, flint hard, baked earth and they could hear and almost feel the little animals' hooves scrape and grind, with each step against the red clay, sometimes sliding as they tried to anchor and fix to it. There was little dust as the bantam mules struggled along in the searing heat, just a low plume, a tiny red puff, not even the height of the little creatures' hooves with each crunching step, the clay particles adhering tightly, to cast the granite hard earth. With each groan of the dry, aged wheels, both end gates were loosely banging against the worn, twisted wood of the floor, jarring the loose, rust covered wagon iron, no longer bolted tight, against the powder dry oak sides of the bed, into high pitched jolting rings.

The old man sat there, jarring with each bounce, dulled and oblivious to the rattle and shaking constantly vibrating through his body. His head atop a gaunt braided rope neck, leathery and extended forward, lordotic with a vulture like curvature. Years behind a plow had caused it, along with causing other deformities and twists not noticed by sight. He always leaned forward, too, while plowing like he was trying to help the mules force the plow through the earth or fleeing a phantom pursuing at his heels trying to seize him. Even when sitting at rest he pitched forward, feet well back under him, neck bent, head erect, as if awaiting some primordial signal or command to flee or commit to battle.

Late, the afternoon of the sixth day, saw them at the edge of the hills. Groaning and jolting of the hard wood and iron continued but the hills, more gradual and gentle now, the little mules were in less of a struggle. Clarence and his sisters still nested in their cushion of hay. The old man and his wife continued to jerk and bounce on their unyielding board seat.

Then there it was. The Delta. They saw it, from the last low rise, fanned out in front of them, to the west, to the north, and southward, too. That warm alluvial soil of the Delta, covered with dark emerald green and smooth as a mural.

A vast ocean of verdant life, spreading toward the sun and beyond the rim of earth itself. The cotton covered plains of the Delta, unbroken, unending, ceaseless and constant. Before them, an unbounded sea of early August cotton, yet green and leafed, but soon to be like a limitless, Siberian tundra, a majestic spread of white. From Georgia, the Carolinas, from Virginia, Tennessee and Kentucky, they had come, onto this fertile alluvial plain, deadened the virgin forest, cleared the impenetrable cane breaks and briars, drained the dark mysterious swamps, then covered the earth with cotton, their immortal sovereign, cotton.

Slowly moving on down into it, down where the cotton was, where the road was dusty and dark. The little mules breathed easier in their heavy gear, their traces not as taut. It was only a dirt trail through a cotton field, but the hills were behind them now. They were going to the west. Dust three inches deep was trampled and pounded by the little beasts' hooves and it rose up under their low swung bellies and on up their flanks and over them to envelop the animals and the wagon and wrap them in a white-gray fog. Worn, iron rimmed, oak wheels lifted it up, too, with each turn and it fell off and drifted in the air. No more red clay, it had disappeared and cotton was bordering each side of the narrow road. It wasn't long before they were several miles into the flat land. Distant hills behind them stretching north and south as far as they could see.

Long shadows stretched rapidly toward the east and would be drawn soon, into darkness and pull the night in around them. The shape of the wagon and its occupants spread in a thin narrow band, straight back toward the hills, like steel cables trying to hold them there, to pull them back toward hunger and futility. An orange-red sun was getting low with the late afternoon. It sat there on the horizon and spread fire across the top of the cotton plants. A bright, orange-red fire, that soon faded into a dark glowing crimson. It continued down below the rim where the sky drained into the earth, drawing the fire toward it, while it sat there throbbing, pulling the fire from across the fields, to descend into darkness and oblivion.

Each five or six miles they would pass through a small town, some with only one or two stores and not many more houses, but all seemed to have a cotton gin. Most gins were two story framed buildings, with a seed pipe coming out of one end leading to a smaller building, a tall smoke stack coming from a side room and a sucker pipe hanging from up in the roof of a lean to, on the opposite side. Most of these were two stand gins powered by a steam engine and ginning only two or three bales an hour. Plantations of any size had a gin and by August there was a huge pile of wood stacked high by the room with the smoke stack, used to fire the engine all fall and winter, if needed.

The stand was the functional unit of the gin, the untangling of the ancient, unyielding mystery of mechanically separating the seed from the cotton fibers. Veritably a support bench or stand, made almost entirely of wood, with a six foot steel shaft of closely placed circular, long toothed saws lying across it. These teeth, when rotating, achieved the same purpose as the long claws of Eli Whitney's cat, which he saw pulling feathers from a chicken through the narrow openings of a wire fence. Thin curved steel strips or ribs spaced between each saw, acted as the wire fence or ribs through which the circular saws projected. Then, the cotton, like the feathers caught in the cat's claws, adhering to the long teeth of the circular rotating saws, was pulled free of the seed through the narrow openings, between the ribs. The bare seed, too big to pass through the openings, dropped into a chute below and the cotton fibers were removed from the saws by more rapidly rotating circular brushes, to be blown into a collection pipe, then to the press and made into a bale.

The first gins were only a small two by four foot box. The mechanism turned by a single hand crank, operated by one man but he could separate more fiber from its seed than one hundred workers could by hand.

Having spent years of study and research on this enigma, with untold, agonizing hours of pondering and meditating on it and being an acute observer, Mr. Whitney's viewing of the cat's actions with the chicken immediately gave him the answer to his search. The answer that changed the world. He then only had to devise a mechanism to mimic the cat's operation. Whereas anyone else seeing this convergence of a clawed feline and a feathered fowl, through a wire fence would only conclude that he had seen a naughty, though hungry, cat and a foolish, though fortunate, chicken. Once again proving the correctness of Pasteur's dictum: "Opportunity favors a prepared mind."

Eli Whitney's epochal scrutiny of the cat's encounter with the chicken, through the wire fence and his simple invention derived from it, has had a more profound impact on the course of human history than any other observation in the record of man. There could be one exception, however, that being, Paris' viewing of Helen, in Sparta, during the Twelfth Century B.C.

The family's journey continued on, clattering and jolting across the widest part of the Delta, hills north of Greenwood to Rosedale. It took nearly three weeks drifting from Tallahatchie County to the swamp settlement, nearly a week out of the hill country, then two weeks or more across the Delta. With few roads marked and no map, they were like migrating animals herded in a certain direction and by instinct alone, kept going.

Just north of Moorhead, where the southern crosses the dog, they came to a wide field of cotton, clear in all directions and for more than nearly a mile to the west they saw no trees or ditch banks or sloughs, only level green cotton that merged into the sky. Soon out of the distant north they saw a train enter their view. It kept getting longer as the boxcars seemed to unravel out of the distance, speeding toward the south. Soon it was almost streaking across the entire horizon spread in front of them. The children had never seen a train and they looked wide eyed, fearful and anxious as they crouched down in the hay. The old man told them, "That ain't nuttin but a train." They had seen pictures of one in an old newspaper and were soon awed enough to stand up in the wagon, holding onto their seated parents.

It was too far away to hear, but they saw the black smoke rush out of the front of it, bend straight back and lay like a cord along the upper parts of the fleeing image, spreading and widening as it hurried toward the end of the train to melt away and dissolve into the air and disappear. They saw a sudden white plume on the top of the engine and in a short time they heard a loud shrill screech like a bobcat wail, off in the woods. It continued a short time, even after the white plume had vanished. "What's that, Papa?" the boy impulsively asked as he held onto his father's shoulder a little tighter. "That's hits whistle," the old man answered. "Hits blowin' for dat crossin' up yonder." The boy thought it looked like a surprised black squirrel, tail straight out behind it in a low, hard run, lined out toward a tree. He could see the wheels as only a blur and he wondered how it was moving with nothing pulling it and what road was it on. They all continued to stare, the mules oblivious to the faint distant image.

The boy, his hand still tight on the old man's shoulders, in total amazement and stunned disbelief, unconsciously babbled, "Papa, das a train." Waiting awhile, the old man gave a low grunt. "Yup." After a pause, the boy asked again, "Whars hit agoin', Papa?" "Hits agoin' on that track yonder." "There's smoke comin' outa hit, ain't it, Papa?" Before he could answer, the boy said again, "Hit must be afar, ain't it, Papa?" "Naw, hit ain't jus sayin' afar, that's hits chimney the smoke's comin' outa." That seemed to satisfy the boy a few seconds, as all four continued to watch the streaking marvel. But, he wondered what would they need a "far" for at this time of year.

Then, when the train had nearly passed, the boy asked again, "Papa, how do hit know, when hit gits to whar hit's agoin'?" With his eyes still fixed on the train, the old man slowly answered, "Son, thar's a man in hit." The boy didn't change his stare. "A man in hit," he later said, "were drivin' hit like I drives this har wagon," the old man said. "Whar's his mules, Papa?" "Ain't no mules, son. Some of 'em says hits got oron horses in hit, though." After awhile, the boy still gazing toward the train, mumbled. "Oron—wonder whar they is?"

They continued west to Rosedale and north on No. 1 to the settlement. With their few household goods in the wagon and the grass hay, the effort was not as much for the little mules on the level Delta roads. Each night a cornfield or garden provided a place to stop, the mules being hobbled and grazed along the roadside.

At the swamp settlement they lived in a side room with an uncle and picked cotton that fall and the old man cut wood from the swamp and peddled it. By spring they had a tenant house and had started a tenant's crop.

After five years in the Delta, his family situation had changed but little and that for the worse. The Wilbanks family had all worked hard fighting the sun, the grass, and the mosquitoes, but they were still living in a tenant cabin, on a Delta cotton farm over close to the river, competing with landless field hands.

As the boy, Clarence, grew older he was always shorter than the rest, but more rotund and globular. Because of his size, he got a new name. "Pig." He was a likable, good natured boy, always ready with a grin and a quick tale. Often, even though the tale was self demeaning, he was the first to laugh.

"Pig" was a regular court jester, ready to entertain and do anything to get somebody's attention and hold it.

In school, too, a few months during the year, he was always the class clown, but to avoid punishment for some misfired prank he would spontaneously, almost by reflex, conjure up a tale, accusing another student of the mischief he had done and with convincing, impeccable assurance, guarantee the teacher of his innocence.

This talent was drilled and practiced more than any class work. Soon it was refined and sharpened and the more it was used the more convincing his smile. Soon it was a part of him, just like his hands and feet. He had an explanation or an alibi for everything. The boy learned and played and with a gleaming broad grin talked his way out of numerous paddlings. But, there was something he could never grin away. The grass in that cotton field. The only thing to rid the field of this was a hoe and it was not self energized. He had to man it. Pig soon tired of hoeing cotton in the boiling sun all summer, then picking it under the same sun during the fall and on into the cold of winter. They had to get all the white fiber, for his family's survival depended on it.

They had survived in the Delta, though, and their existence had been much more than bearable. Pig usually got one or two pairs of new overalls each year, several shirts, shoes if he had outgrown his old ones, and when needed he always had a coat and something to cover his head. His family had enough to eat, though they grew most of it. Usually working in the fields only four or five months during the year and then, certainly not every day, their existence was much easier and believably freer than ninety percent of the people in the country who were not farmers. A few months in the cotton field each year, though most of it in summer, with plenty to eat year round was certainly less tiring than 12 months of 12 hour days, five and a half to six days a week, every week, endured by factory and textile mill workers, tied to a loom or spinning machine or some other work station, only to subsist with a meager existence. He had said for a long time, though, "My hands don't fit dat hoe," and he wanted out of the jailed confinement that was the cotton field.

For Pig this action was too slow. The old man gave him some money once a year when he sold his cotton and the 35 cents a day he got for working in a neighbor's field, the few days he was not in his own, would buy very little that he could display or flaunt. He wanted to have some money, some cash money. Money he could see and feel and count, his guardian against yearning and fear. Money he could show somebody.

"You know, money's all they is," he told his mother. "Everything else ain't nothin' but talk." His mother, however, had warned him repeatedly that, "Money weren't for you, son. For no man. It bore the signs of Satan." Her family and his father's family and all their blood kin had for years, for eons past, never had any money, nor if they did they could not keep it to acquire land or any place except a back water squatter's swamp or the poorest, most worthless piece of abandoned hillside earth.

Since the dawn of man, when the first aboriginal came down from the trees, their fate had been to be the beggars, the paupers, the thieves and laborers, the barn burners and hog stealers, the human dregs of the earth. With subsistence living for so many generations, they knew that was all there was or should be, in this life and the most they ever wanted was to arrive at this with the least effort. They had ennobled poverty and dignified it, made it inviolable, holy and righteous, made it God's blessed state. It was sanctified as religion and their defeat, one of its precepts. In this black soil of hopelessness and despair, there was a fear of life, a sloven, shiftless indolence with an attitude of fatalism. To have a few belongings and little money was the goal, but anything more than I have is unchristian and profane heathenism, only done or accomplished by a damnable, hell bound, Faustian compact with Satan.

But, Pig had seen some money, stacks of silver dollars some tenants had gotten when they sold their cotton. He had seen what it would buy and he wanted it. He would worry about Satan later on.

He knew his mother had said and the preachers had preached on the evils of it. "The fraudulent path to all pleasure and peace." He had heard the preacher say how a rich man would never get to the Lord. He had heard him preach on the "wickedness of it, the iniquity and the devilry of it." He then heard him holler just before he was out of breath and nearly choked down, "It bore the sulfurous stink of damnation. Even too much time thinking about it, would bind you to Satan and to hell." Then he prayed for salvation from its corruption, its immorality and its hell bound sinfulness, all the while he was crying as he preached and prayed on it and the whole church cried. The preacher then turned right around and passed the plate and asked for it.

His mother constantly annoyed and irritated the old man, about his never going to the tiny, cypress shingled church, where he could hear the preacher, except for the rare funeral or a night or two during the summer to a protracted meeting. "You need to go hear the word of the Lord preached," she told him, "talk to him and sing to him." "Why, I can talk to him right here, right here in this field," he said. "Don't the Bible say he's ever where?" "Yeah, he's ever where, but the preachin's good, will open up yer eyes so's you can see 'im better and the singin's good," she said. "You'd like the singin'." "Them folks over there ain't asingin'," he answered. "They ain't doin' nothin' but hollerin'."

Then, she told him, "Brother Hannah can pray, too. Why, he can offer a prayer, sweet as anything you ever heard. It'd do you good just to hear 'im." "Sweet to you," he said. "Why, he wudna prayin' to you, was he?" "Naw," the old woman answered, "but it sho is good just to hear 'im. He has some of 'em shoutin' and hollerin', some cryin', he'll put the fear of the Lord in you." "Why, the Lord don't want nobody with fear in him," the old man answered. "He don't want no hollerin' and cryin'. He's seen enough of dat already. All dat scared and cryin'. The Lord don't want nobody 'fraid. Why, he ain't gonna terrify nobody." "Why, a sinner orta be scared," she answered. "Yeah, that's right, he orta be scared," the old man said, "but dat's the very one that ain't scared or he wouldn't be asinnin'.

The Lord wants forgivin' if a man needs it, and love and feelin' good. He don't want the people tremblin' and runnin' and ahollerin." "Brother Hannah don't say nuthin about nobody arunnin', she soon answered.

"I knowed he prob'ly did'n, but if they git scared, that's sho what they gonna do. I don't care about that preacher's prayin.' I'll do my own talkin' to the Lord. That preacher can't talk to the Lord for me. I'll do my own talkin' long as I can say somethin'. Would you want somebody acomin' and talkin' to you about somebody else's business?" he asked. "Naw, you would'n. I got time to do my own talkin' and I ain't gonna bother 'im all the time with it, either, like I hear's that preacher adoin'.

Why, that preacher over there's got a necktie on, up there showin' off. He ain't no necktie preacher. He ain't got no biznis wearin' no necktie like them big city preachers. I sez he ain't doin' nothin' but hollerin' and scarin' the people. With that necktie on, he look like a jersey bull in a thicket with a bell on." "He don't always wear no tie," she interrupted. "Mostly when he's apreachin' he does," the old man answered, "and when he ain't got one on up there hollerin' he's got atere sunflower tie clasp pinned on 'im tryin' to fool somebody like he knows what to do. That don't make him no preacher, wearing all athat."

That was the usual field talk with Pig right there listening to it all, though he heard very little. The old man and his wife seemed to thrive on it. Their rows were cleaned with the hoe much quicker and night seemed to come earlier.

One afternoon late toward the end of their field talk, the old man finally said, "I's gonna find me a preacher dat tells the truf, dat makes a man feel good 'bout de Lord. I don't want no hollerin' and tremblin' and scared. I'll know hit, too, when I hear 'im." He added slowly. "How you gonna know hit?" she said. "You don't know nothin' 'bout the Bible." "I do know 'bout the Bible. I heared it tells the truf and when I hear dat, I'll feel good and know hit, too, 'cause hit won't be somethin' away off yonder somewheres. It'll be right cheer. It'll be like you dun found somethin' you been lookin' a long time for and it won't be nothin' scared and tremblin' either. It'll be somethin' natural to a man and he might feel somethin' pass over 'im like he's settin' on his front porch or like he's settin' in his own house or like he's off in the woods somewheres ahuntin'. I heared a preacher like that once when I was a boy. I know I'll sho'ly hear another one."

Pig was right there with them during these conversations, he and his two sisters, each hoeing their grass laden rows. Occasionally one of the girls would ask a question. All three of the children went to the church with their mother and hearing the preacher, the girls were usually too afraid to ask very much and were always given an answer, heightening their fear and silencing them.

Pig was deaf to all this fluster of field talk whirling and churning back and forth around him. He only heard one thing. He had to get out of this cotton field to get some money. There were things he wanted, things that took money to buy. He found a Sears and Roebuck catalog, an old one someone had given his mother. He read it all, first page to the last, studied and pondered each page and each picture, then for hours he puzzled over each of them. He read and fantasized about what he saw and brooded over the wonders and images like the preacher studied and dwelled on his Bible. He knew each page, all of them, not just the parts that added to his hunger and his illusions, but the wonders he saw there and the voices he heard from the catalog, from the pictures and the pages. He heard each one. He knew what they said to him. He knew he could have what he saw in that book and that was what he called it.

Pig's work in the field did not distract him from his thoughts and his fantasies of his book. Even when the old man rode him hard and tongue lashed him about his sloven, grubby hoeing. He called him a dreamer and said he was "no 'count" and told him he would "never 'mount to nothing." That didn't disturb him in the least. He kept dreaming. His work never improved.

He studied it even at night with the light of a kerosene lamp. He knew every item in it, from the three dollar shotgun to the two dollar and twenty-five cent boy's suit, which included the cap. He knew all the pictures and what was written under them. He had spent hours studying each one. With his fingers pressed against each slick, smooth page, he slowly felt each picture, his fingers outlining them as they moved over the paper, and he drew them with his fingertips and he could close his eyes and see the images as he felt them glide beneath his fingers, knowing each word written beneath them and the cost of every one.

Pressing his fingers over the pages, he said, "I could zern um," and he was sure he owned them all. Each night he felt the shotgun, opened the breach, put a shell in it, took a slow aim, at a squirrel, atop an 80 foot pecan and fired. Then, after awhile, on to the other pictures. When the lamp light was gone or when he was in the field, he probed his pictures and words again, examining and mining each page and each image, pulling and prying from them all the details of value and pleasure, each nugget, his memory could surmise. Pig had long ago decided he would have some of the things he saw. They would not always be a dream. He thought, too, that he would never find them in his daddy's cotton field and hoeing cotton at thirty cents a day he would never be able to have that shotgun.

Cotton prices had begun to rise a little since the great war had started in Europe, and each year since 1914 the old man's cotton had been sold for a few cents more. The family was now picking twelve to fourteen bales a year with the family's part being one-half of that. Their money had begun to increase, but their living costs increased with it. An occasional newspaper, from Memphis, would find its way to the swamp settlement. This was about all they knew of the war. But, the fall armistice was signed, the old man's cotton was sold for twenty cents a pound.

Cotton farming began to look better. There was an occasional car on the road since the war. The store at the settlement had more to sell. Pig's mother and two sisters bought a new Sunday dress. The girls' cost a dollar seventy-five each. He got a new jumper, a pair of overalls, and a new pair of shoes.

The next spring they planted two more acres of cotton and they heard that cotton would be 25 cents that fall. They planted a new kind of cotton on the two acres they added that spring, a variety called "Doctor Wilds." It would bring more money, supposed to have an inch and a half staple.

The crop got off to a good start that spring. The rains came when the young plants needed them and the old man and his family were able to keep the grass whipped back. It was a struggle, though. The assault of the hoe set upon the fury of a virulent array of mid summer Delta grass was at times an uneven battle fought only to a stalemate. Sometimes they would chop it down late in the afternoon, only to find that some of the grass had sprouted roots and was again green and fresh, growing the next morning. They grappled on in the fierce heat of the long summer and by the Fourth of July their skirmish with the grass, the mosquitoes, and the heat was coming to an end. Though they had about three more weeks in the field, they had fought the grass to a draw. The shade of the rank cotton did the rest. They had endured the mosquitoes and managed to survive the omnipotence of the sun.

They did not go to the field on the Fourth. None of their neighbors did. An ice truck came down from Clarksdale several times that summer and they had some ice they had bought the week before. Ten cents bought them fifty pounds. It was kept in a buried wooden barrel surrounded by a thick wall of sawdust, a small shed built over the entire assemblage. For the first time that Fourth they had something cold to drink.

Pig and his sisters could not believe it. They had some cheese, too, from the store. There was a hoop of it there, covered in a coating of black wax, that had come from Wisconsin by way of a wholesale grocery company in Memphis, then by steamboat to the landing. The children had never seen cheese before. When they first ate it, the younger sister cried for it all night. That summer they had something cold to drink, that wasn't pump water lemonade and they had hoop cheese. The old woman fried chicken and they went to a picnic in a grove behind the church yard. From noon until night there was "gittar pickin' and fiddlin' and hollerin'" until the mosquitoes and heat in the heavy still air of the grove finally ran them home.

Two or three more weeks in the field and they would lay by, spending the time until picking in middle to late August, getting in hay for the mules and cow and canning vegetables from their garden. When they lived in the hills, they would always lay by on the Fourth or before, but this Delta grass was of another mind and they had to hack away at it sometimes until August.

The old man had heard talk several times during the summer that cotton prices were going up in Memphis and cotton might be even twenty-six or twenty-seven cents that fall, but they had heard this kind of talk before and nobody paid much attention.

As the long, extended days and brief nights of summer fitfully shuttled and burned through August and slowly crept into September, the leaves of the cotton plants rapidly dried and falling to the ground, left the big full bolls to be blasted open by the continued long days, of sun and its sweltering torrid fire. Waiting for the field to turn white, and with much less work to do, Pig and his old man spent several hours each day loitering around the store, where there were always other tenants and occasionally a plantation owner would ride by and mix in the crowd.

The three Williamson brothers, who had just the year before, bought another big place, two thousand acres they said, were frequently there and were the center of most of the talk. Thad, the youngest, had boasted to the crowd that they would probably buy another thousand acres that fall.

The talk was always about crops, usually cotton and the weather. Rains had come about the right time during the spring and summer and most of the farmers had better than average fields. Each day or so rumors came from Clarksdale or even Memphis about the price of cotton and most weeks there was talk of the price rising. When they started picking, word had come down, that cotton was nearly thirty-five cents in Memphis.

The next week, even before they were all in the white fields, one of the Williamson brothers came by the store and told the crowd that his man in Memphis said cotton would sell for forty cents that fall.

Pig and his family were a work force now, there were five of them, all nearly grown. His oldest sister could pick nearly as much as he could. The five of them, in the field sometimes even before the dew was off and working until dark, would pick two and a half bales of cotton a week. On during the pretty fall they continued to hear the revelations from Memphis, of higher prices. The first week in October the youngest Williamson declared at the store one morning, "Cotton can now be sold for fifty cents."

Pig was eighteen that fall and hearing all this talk about the price rising, the cotton field began to look a little better. He started to dream that he might be able to find some money there. He still had his "book" and as he got older he studied it even more than before, still slowly moving his fingers over the pictures, dreaming and reciting the words under each of them.

By mid October they had finished picking their fields. They had twelve bales, two of them the "Doctor Wilds" long staple cotton. His family were tenants, however. The land belonged to another man and he decided when to sell the cotton, all of it, and the price he would take for it. The landowner got one-half of the cotton. Pig's family got the other half, but had to pay their living expenses out of that.

In early November the landowner sold half of the cotton for sixty cents a pound. Pig's family got part of that, paid their living expenses for the year. All their profit, their pocket money, their money to spend and buy things with, money for winter clothes and food and the old man thought, maybe a second hand Model T Ford, all this was in their half of the cotton not yet sold. This included their bale of "Doctor Wilds" they had hoed and plowed and carefully picked and cared for like a garden.

The "Doctor Wilds" cotton was pretty all right. It was shoulder high when it was picked and covered with bolls. They carefully picked every lock of it, despite the thorn sharp burrs around each boll. Even though it took eighteen hundred to two thousand pounds of the picked cotton to make a five hundred pound bale, they ginned two bales off of their two acre patch.

The old man and Pig had seen the landowner pull the cotton, to straighten the fibers to see and measure their length and, seeing this a few times, Pig was quick to learn how to pull the soft staple. He had pulled it a hundred times and become expert at it. Holding a tuft of the cotton between each thumb and forefinger, he would slowly separate his thumbs, holding a small bit of cotton in each hand. Then rolling his fixed fingers, straightening some of the fibers, he would overlay that held in one hand onto the other, then pull again. With a few pulls and overlays, the long, immaculately white, pristine and unblemished fibers would become straight as a plumbed line and lay parallel side by side, dense and compact, almost one and a half inches long. He would then take his time, for a long look at the white, soft fiber and feel it softly pressed between his thumb and fingers. Then, cupping the cotton in his hand, he would place it against his nose and slowly sniff it, letting it linger there awhile, then leisurely inhale again, before releasing it, to float on the warm air, the slight sharp odor, distinctive and clear, rapidly filling his brain.

With talk of prices still rising, they knew their bale of "Doctor Wilds" and two bales of the short staple cotton would bring them more money than they had ever seen before, or that they had ever heard about. The old man said he may not have to work another year and Pig felt increasingly better about his money as he continued his catalog studies.

That fall crept by slow and warm, with little rain, but the cool nights and early mornings brought a frequent frost. During the warm, sunny October days, the whole earth and sky and the very air itself, had been filled with a brightness, different from any that summer, for the dark emerald green of spring and July and August, that absorbed all the sunlight had turned to a sunny yellow and orange, golden and crimson red, absorbing none of the brightness but reflecting it back and dispersing it, to be bounced again and again, a thousand times from golden leaf to golden leaf and back to bright crimson, coercing the whole countryside and the swamp into becoming brighter than summer and even clearer, a definite outline or margin shown on each stalk and leaf and blade of grass. With more colors than could be seen, any other time of year, the swamp at times was afire with a radiant brilliance and when the fields were white, the magic of the colors played on the cotton, giving it a different light, but wrapped still in a hue of pure whiteness with the tone of a more subdued glow and a more defined luster.

The swamp lay to the north and was a dark golden to deep crimson in late afternoon. There in the distance, a jay made his last call of the day. A panther bawled deep in the woods, to the west over toward the river. A hawk circled low overhead. Stalks in a tall grass patch trembled, as a rabbit silently crept through and the survivors slept with an alertness, as the fires were banked into night.

The old man and Pig began to wonder about their money and had talked to the landowner several times, but he had not sold anymore cotton, yet holding, for a higher price.

Pig and the old man went to the store the first week of December where they heard cotton was eighty cents in Memphis. There was the usual crowd at the store that day, farmers, tenants, sharecroppers, but none were talking about selling any of their crop. A scant number, however, had sold theirs but they were close-mouthed about it, just listening, wondering if they had sold too low. Most, however, were holding for higher prices, what price they did not know, but just higher, even though in only nine months it had gone up more than five hundred percent.

There was talk that morning that old man Shaw had sold his entire crop, ninety bales, at seventy-eight cents and paid off all his debts, his land now in the clear. His tenants, even, had a little money. But several in the crowd mentioned how foolish he had been, giving his cotton crop away. They talked about the price of cotton daily. With little work to do now in the early winter months, the local crowd met at the store daily, afraid to miss some sale signal or revelation that would be proclaimed there.

As the days and weeks passed and Christmas gradually moved closer, they only became more anxious, hearing of the price's continued rise. After fifteen cent cotton the year before, and even much less, in any man's memory, with this sharp rise to almost ninety cents now, most knew it certainly would go even higher, propelled upward by an unseen and unknown but righteous and justifiable, even legitimate force, to make right an entitlement, for the years of deprivation and ceaseless toil.

Though there had been several sharp downward breaks during the late summer and early fall, it was widely rumored that this was only the manipulations of some Wall Street money pools to scare some of the cotton out on the market. They knew it would continue up, and it did. Several of the sharecroppers and land owners gave their opinion on the international situation causing the higher prices.

Old Joe Brown rose out of his seat that morning and loudly asserted, "I read an article where it said all the cotton was dyed khaki or olive drab and used up, what waddin' burnt up in artillery shells, during the war. Thar ain't no more cotton in the worl'. Why, cotton may go to five dollars. Ya'll know they got to have cotton. They say hits important as iron." Joe got only a few wide eyed glances for that, but somebody answered, "It sho is. Ain't I been tellin' ya'll dat?" Another voice added, "Our cotton's better than them furiners' anyway." Every man there who had not yet sold his cotton knew it would only continue its upward spiral.

About two weeks before Christmas on a Friday afternoon, Thad walked in the store and while standing in the middle of the crowd casually announced, "I jus' left Mr. Holland at the Bank of Clarksdale. He said cotton'll be a dollar and a quarter in two weeks."

A sudden hush fell over the crowd and they all stared at Thad in open mouthed amazement. Some could not believe it. They had never heard of cotton at that price. But, that banker in Clarksdale knew what he was talking about and Thad had brought them the news. Then, one of the small farmers announced, "I knowed it. I sho' knowed it. Aint I been tellin' ya'll dat?" Another responded, "That's 'bout what I figgered. I been sayin' that all along." They all seemed satisfied. But, more than that, relieved and thankful, as they finally knew, after months of anguish, at what price they would get to sell a year's work, the value of a year of toil and effort, a year of deprivation and struggle. They knew now the price they would get for their cotton crop. Mr. Holland, at the Bank of Clarksdale, had set the price and the youngest Williamson brother had brought it to them. The crowd gave an appreciative, amazed look toward Thad, who was eager to accept his due adoration. He stood there for awhile, leaning against the counter, a smirkish grin on his face, fixing glances with each man as they dutifully nodded toward him, their motions just short of a bow.

Thad knew cotton was going up. He had known it for six or eight months now. Mr. Holland at the bank had told him in the spring that cotton was going up, that it would be a good price in the fall and he saw it continue to rise since that time just like the banker said, slowly at first, but the price during the past two months had almost exploded upward.

They would be able to pay off their new place, he thought, as he stood there showing his slick grin, and probably pick up another thousand acres, maybe even another two thousand. Times were good and they better get that land while they could.

"Well, boys," he cocked his head again, "we'll have a good Christmas this year."

After awhile he gazed around the room and with a quick grin and rapid short motion of his head, he started toward the door. The crowd of grateful sharecroppers and small farmers slowly parted, opening a path he followed through the door and then swaggered across the porch to mount his big horse tied there. They all rapidly filled the porch behind him.

Before he rode away, he stood his big horse and facing them again, he tightened the reins. The animal's head swung straight up as he stood in the stirrups and like a triumphant general, returned them a wide, waving salute and approvingly accepted their obvious admiration. "Well, boys, it's a new day now," he loudly declared. "Times will be good. You better get you some more land. They done fixed it." He waved again. "Cotton'll be here forever."

The crowd watched him as he rode off. Thad never looked back, but he knew they were all there. He held the reins a little tight and touched a spur to the big horse's side. The animal immediately went into a fast racking gait, smooth as a rocking chair, his back and hips in a slow vibration. The crowd saw this and hollered. They all felt better than they had in months. "Boy, look at that big horse single foot," one yelled. Thad didn't look back, but threw his arm up and waved once more. As he rapidly moved on down the road, a loud roar came up again from the crowd.

Thad thought about buying another two or three thousand acres as he rode home. They would need a gin with that much land and they could certainly get plenty outside ginning. The oil mill would lend the money to build one. Then, another couple of thousand acres and they would have one of the biggest plantations in the Delta, except for the syndicate and they weren't Delta people anyway, Englishmen owned that. He thought about his older age when he would sit on a wide columned front porch, owning the land as far as he could see and beyond. He may even get into politics and be elected to the senate where he could do some real good. First, he would get on home and tell his brothers about Mr. Holland's prediction and advice.

Late in October Thad had openly speculated that he and his brothers would buy another two thousand acres. By mid November they had fifteen hundred bales stacked around their commissary and were offered seventy-eight cents for it, just three weeks before Christmas.

It was late that afternoon when Thad got home, after his announcement at the store, of the banker's prediction and found his brothers talking to a cotton buyer from Clarksdale. He had offered them eighty cents a pound for the fifteen hundred bales. Their bookkeeper was there and he figured at that price they could pay off their entire mortgages on all their land. About the time the bookkeeper told them that, Thad burst in and announced again, "I just left Mr. Holland at the Bank of Clarksdale and he said cotton would be a dollar and a quarter in two weeks." The brothers called the cotton buyer every kind of scandal and crook they could think of, for trying to steal their cotton. The buyer got on his horse in a hurry and left for Clarksdale. Thad had cried out the Clarksdale banker's prediction twice that same afternoon and he was confident and jubilant that he had prevented his brothers and the other farmers from giving away their cotton.

Thad and his brothers had moved there from over in Webster County about the time the boll weevils came. His oldest brother who had a year at A&M got a job as a plantation rider and soon sent for his two younger brothers. Thad had gotten a job as a store clerk and his other brother followed the oldest as a rider. Thad had done well as a clerk. He worked hard, from early until late and he could always sell a tenant something, whether he needed it or not. The store owner liked him and knew the hard working young man had a good future and he helped Thad buy his first forty acres. Thad put two tenants on the forty who planted it all in cotton. He was able to keep his job full time at the store. He worked even harder then and rode out to his place only at night and on Sundays, spending the daylight hours, six days a week, in the store. In several more years he had a hundred sixty acres, all paid for. Owed nothing on it, no mortgage, it was "in the clear." His brothers, too, had saved their money and were buying about two hundred acres together. It wasn't completely paid for yet, but they were working hard on it. This is the land they mortgaged just the year before, to buy the two thousand acres of good sandy ground. Thad's land, however, that went into the mortgage as collateral was the only part that was debt free.

Thad continued working in the store and the two older brothers managed the place. To "work out" their part, they had no trouble filling it up with labor, for most of the tenants were already there when they bought it. About the first of June, though, Thad could stay away no longer and he left the store to ride with his brothers.

The Williamson brothers knew how to grow cotton and Thad was quick to give his neighbors advice. They had grown up in Webster County. Their family had a small cotton farm next to Tom Bailey's folks' place. The Williamson boys and Tom were good friends, had played and later hunted together. Tom had, however, gone to A&M for four years, then to law school. He went on later to live in the Governor's mansion in Jackson. The Williamson boys came to the Delta. During the oldest brother's year at A&M he had taken "Southern Field Crops" and "Introduction to Agronomy," among other things. This certainly qualified all of them to be the best farmers in the area, or so Thad repeatedly told his friends.

After the cotton buyer left on his fort horse, Thad, his brothers and their bookkeeper sat around their wood fired, hot office stove in the back of their commissary for several hours. They all were elated. They would pay off their new place, the balance on the older brother's two hundred and Thad would again own his hundred and sixty. Their years of hard work had been worth all the toil and effort. The two older brothers just sat close to the heater. They would have some time off from their wrenching months long wait and worry. Thad was up walking from the heater to a window back to a desk in constant motion. He had told them cotton was going up, now it had. "Cotton will be here," he told his brothers. "We got to fix for it." After awhile they all went home. That night they slept the quiet, easy sleep of a child.

That night a cold December rain started. The long crop gathering season had ended. Most had been finished, however, for weeks and were not at the store but were hunting quail. There were several days of blowing winter rain, nearly a week. Then the week before Christmas, a crowd gathered at the store again. Thad never showed up or any of the Williamson brothers, but someone else had heard that cotton was now sixty cents in Memphis. A few days before Christmas, someone from Clarksdale said they heard it was fifty-four cents. But, they all knew it was certain to go back up.

All that winter they waited and it did surge up and down a little, just enough to spark some hope, but never enough for any other farmers to sell. The general trend was always down. The Delta winter raged on, and so did the gloom and the somber brooding. There were a few warm days to hunt or walk to the store, but most of the daylight hours over the next four weeks were usually spent around the fireplace or stove at home, with only an hour or so outside each day, to feed and water animals.

During a rare trip to the store in early February, Pig and the old man heard that some cotton had been sold for twelve cents a pound. Thad was at the store that morning just sitting there, staring at the hot stove with the rest of the crowd. They saw him as they walked in and noticed he never looked up when they slammed the door shut. There was a dull absence to his abandoned stare and he had a defenseless, forlorn, defeated cast surrounding him, not just his facial expression but his entire body, the tilt of his head and shoulders, his hand motions and the angle of his bent slouch in the chair, together the picture of desperate hopelessness. When asked a question, there was only an occasional grunt or "could'n tell ya." He would come by the store, sit and stare at the stove for hours, which was the same preoccupation of most of the usual crowd.

Occasionally when someone had an unusually successful bird or rabbit hunt he would come by the store to tell the crowd. All other sparse conversation was still the price of cotton. "Wonder how long hits agoin' down? When hits agoin' back up?" By now, most of the store sitters had even a different walk and stride, too, changed from the rapid quickness of the fall. They seemed to walk with a slow uncertainty, insecure and seemingly careless and confused about where they may be going. Staring at the stove or even talking to a friend, their faces grim and somber, lined with an awed disbelief and puzzlement which seemed more and more to show itself as the days agonizingly churned on and slowly struggled and trudged into weeks. Their eyes big and dilated with the raw, hungry face of fear, abject, immutable fear, sinister and unspeakable, like they never saw what was in front of them but were only staring at something distant and far away, something they could not see and did not know, but something they knew was morbid and merciless, against which they had no counter or defense. A few adopted a strange aloofness, were isolated and seldom seen, staying at home, like they were holed up there, hiding in a cold house, at night, off in a side room, to a colder bed. When they were at the store, however, there was a hostility and standoffishness about them and when approached by a friend, there was only a quick answer, with a sideways embarrassed glance, as if ashamed to be seen like their neighbors, broke and destitute. Most of the loud voices, of that jubilant fall, they had all reveled in were now muted and there was little talk in the store anymore.

Thad came by the store again in late January. After standing quietly awhile, with outstretched hands toward the heat of the stove, he looked up across the crowd with a dazed, indifferent stare toward the light of a west window and in a detached, distraught voice he absentmindedly murmured, "It's goin' to be tough on us planters. I don't know how you little boys gonna make it." He stared there toward the light another minute, then turned and walked slowly toward the door and his horse. They all turned to look at him but none followed. Several spit on the hot stove and watched it sizzle and steam, spreading its scorched rank vapor in the air.

With each short upward surge in the cotton price, hope would flare again and they thought maybe this is it, the price would go back up. This never happened. The trend was down and steep. A few had sold their crop near the peak, but most were hoping and listening to word from the Clarksdale banker and Thad, had not sold any. Some of the older men had a more desperate forlorn appearance, solemn and stone faced, like an escaped convict after a long run, finally cornered and surrounded by hounds or a posse, brought down at last by a force beyond their reach.

Some of those less desperate, those farmers without much debt, were not totally consumed by despair and still had not abandoned hope. They had never had anything but a roof, it might leak, and usually enough to eat. They had wrested their land from a swamp, cleared it and drained it, survived the crash of 1895, the high water of 1897, fought malaria every year, endured the deadly yellow fever of 1878, sent their families to Memphis or the hills in summer, but did not abandon the land. "Long as we can feed our mules and tenants and get a little credit at the store for tobacco and coffee, we'll be here. May have to plant some of that new long staple cotton, though, that "Dr. Wills," old man Shaw said at the store one morning. They would try again. The land was still there.

February started cold. During the first week a mid winter sky turned iron gray, dull and gloomy for the short daylight hours. After a day or two of this overcast, leaden skies grew darker and ashen, with no sun, even at noon. Wind came hard from the northwest and colder. Temperatures dropped twenty-five degrees one afternoon and a few scattered snow flurries blew in later. By next morning, gray sunless skies were filled with whirling snow. Pig couldn't see the barn and never left the fireplace all day. His mother, the old man and two sisters all sat staring in the fire from their segment of circle around the hearth, leaving only to get food from a cold kitchen. With the air a dull, granite, gray white swirl, without sun most of the day, shortly after noon the gloom turned to darkness and the blackness to night.

When the snow swirl stopped, they did not know, but when morning came there was an early sun and the land shown white with a foot of snow and the air glistened with the sparkle of tiny crystals. Snow drifts were deep against buildings and trees, against the cotton rows and last year's old stalks. Hushpuckena Creek was frozen solid. A mule walked across it that morning.

A slight warming during the day melted the surface, but darkness again came early and the next morning the surface was frozen, ice pack hard. Again, the sun was up early and it sat just above the horizon, bright and blazing, land to the west, a vast white glitter of sparkle. When Pig tried to walk on it, he found it impossible to stand and he had to crawl to the barn. Snow stayed for nearly two weeks with the temperature in the twenties.

Before the hearth, staring into the yellow flickering glow of an oak blaze one frigid night, their opened hands and faces feeling the fire's warmth while the raw chill against their backs spread out into every corner of the room behind them, resisting even the meager effort of the fire. Pig's youngest sister, bundled in a coat and a sock hat, pulled down low over her ears, happened to turn and see the five shadows flickering on the opposite wall. "Looka there, Momma. Look at our shadows on the wall," she called out. Her mother acted as if she never heard her, but kept staring into the fire. The yellow light hardly struggled off of the bare, wooden walls, but the young eyes could easily see it and the shadows as they moved and turned, with each sudden changing size and shape and flicker of the flames, none similar in any way and no motion the same. She watched the shadows as they played and danced and changed on the wall, as children and philosophers had done for ten thousand years. She made hers take many grotesque shapes and make strange, distorted movements and stretched it taller and bigger than all the others or smaller, even, just by her distance from the fire. She saw that she could totally control it and enlarge it or squeeze it as she chose. She played games with it a long time, making anything she wished and becoming whatever or whomever she desired, enthralled by the illusions, totally oblivious to the searching cold and even to the four other people and the changing fire. This could have been in central Europe during the last Ice Age, in a Neanderthal cave, or in a hut on the chalk downs of Salisbury Plain, in a cave in Attica, or even much later in the Great Hall in Windsor Castle. All the same, save for the illusions, but this was in a cold, Delta, tenant shack on a frigid arctic night.

Never noticing her daughter and without taking her eyes from the flames, Pig's mother asked the old man, "Why don't you go to church and get Brother Hannah to pray, get him to offer a prayer for better prices? He sho offers a good prayer." The old man never answered. She continued, "He might git the Lord to raise prices some. He'll git the Lord to hep us." The old man, still looking at the short leaps and flickers of the yellow blaze, spit in the flames again, then answered, "Why, the Lord done already sent us nearly 'bout eighty-five cents for cotton. Why, ain't no tellin' what that Doctor Wilds woulda brought, maybe a dollar and a quarter. Wid all dat, us little bossman didn' have sense enough to sell it." He spit again in the fire and instantly it sizzled, spreading once more its rank, scorched tobacco odor through the cold air of the room. "Ain't no tellin' what I coulda bought this fall if he hadda sold it." After awhile he turned toward the old woman when he said, "Like I done said, dat necktie preacher don' know nothin' 'bout no prayin'." "All he knows is hollerin'. I believe the Lord's done already heard enougha that." He stared in the fire again and spit, the rank odor effusing rapidly through the room. "I done tol' ya," he added again, "he already done sent eighty-five cent cotton."

February continued cold and on into March. In early March the old man's boss sold his cotton for five and a half cents. The "Doctor Wilds" brought eight.

Banks and insurance companies began calling their loans and cotton farms throughout the Delta were foreclosed. Tenants didn't lose any land, they never had any. Their loss had already happened in the collapse of the price of cotton. Most stayed on the land where they were, making arrangements with the new landowners or the insurance companies or banks' managers.

Talk around the store now was about who had lost their place and "wonder what he's gonna do." Jed Roberts, a small landowner, told a friend one morning when the two of them were alone in the store, "I heard Mr. Berryhill done lost that new place he bought down in Louisiana, that new place he bought for four hundred dollars an acre to grow broom corn and he done lost Mound Plantation, too, his house with it. Wonder where he'll go?" No one knew where the foreclosures would send them. Some of the more fortunate, ruined, bankrupt farmers would move in with a family member, but others were often left to endure in a tenant house again and try to start over, their family back in the field. Occasionally one would find a job in town, given by a merchant whom he had favored, but never by a grocery merchant, for most landowners had their own commissary supplying their tenants and any others willing to trade there.

Thad had not been to the store since his last pronouncement in January. But, there was talk there, that the brothers' land would be lost. In about a week, Jed walked in with the news. "Well, I heard the Williamson boys done lost their place and got to move." The crowd was quiet for awhile, there were only a few grunts and an occasional head shaking. Then, Hozey, a clerk in the store, commented, "Look's like some-a-da big planters done fell, the more substantial people." There'll be more than that what falls afore this thing's over with," Jake Allen answered.

The price collapse devastated the entire south, parts of Texas and California, too. But the Delta felt it worse than any other region of the country. It spread to the mills in the Carolinas and New England, across the Atlantic to the mills in Manchester and the continent, to North Africa and to Asia.

By late fall of that crop year, one bale of cotton at its peak price, eighty-eight cents, which held for about a week, would have bought a new automobile, a Model T Ford. The following spring, to buy the same car took thirty. There was talk around the store that the insurance companies and banks had sold the Williamson brothers' cotton for four and three quarters cents. Four months before, had they sold it, their entire debt would have been paid. The land would have been theirs "free of debt, clear of any liens, owned straight out by the Williamson boys," so the talk went. A good number of cotton farms in the Delta changed hands that winter, but those farmers who survived seemed once again to gather strength and hope and determination from their own survival and endurance and the barrier they had hurdled. Then, with the spring the entire Delta was again planted in cotton.

Some of the larger farmers and plantation owners, that survived, had always managed a good living, but none had accumulated any serious wealth. A few, however, had their land paid for, but had to mortgage a part of it each year in order to produce a new crop. They usually acquired a comfortable home and a car that was easily started, could sometimes go to Oak Hall in Memphis during the fall and buy a new felt hat and a Hickey Freeman suit.

Yet, there was the much publicized, but certainly uncommon, week long trip to New York, reveled in the remainder of the year, until the next trip and it was an infrequent, though memorable, occurrence indeed, when on the front page of the society section of the Memphis paper, there appeared a long column or half page, detailing a Delta planter's returning from a voyage to London or Paris or touring the Mediterranean with stopovers in Rome, the Grecian Isles or Venice.

Returning home, the wife, with the authoritative voice of a classics professor, would give an in depth lecture at her club, for forty-five minutes, on the Minoan and the Athenian civilizations, including their culture, their art, their literature, and their government structure, along with a description of the architectural splendor, the enthralling elegance and the spell binding, magnetic beauty of the relationship of the proportions, or ratio of the dimensions, of the Parthenon. To this she would add the entire history of Venice, encompassing its art and architecture and whether the gondolier was a baritone or tenor. All this with a complete description of St. Mark's Cathedral, the doge's palace, the art within the Academia, the scenery along one hundred seventy miles of canals and the bridges. The history of western civilization from the third millennia B.C. through sixteenth century Venice, plus a detailed account of the form and movements and mellow, soft voice and eye of a living gondolier. Then, tea cakes and coffee, complete and unabridged and awake, all in an hour.

Every area had a small group of flamboyant, ostentatious, exhibitionists, letting everybody in the county know when they had ten dollars and could make a display of a hundred dollars, louder, brighter, and longer than a Broadway stage director or a Fourth of July fireworks display. They could borrow a hundred dollars and put on a bigger, more dazzling display or masquerade than old man Rockefeller would with a million. Most of this stripe, however, would serve only one term.

There was, however, that uncommon inheritor, whose bequeathment, protected by trust or other barrier to his reach was able to spend a lifetime on tour and there being mesmerized by that crowd, its regalia and consumption, attracted to and cognizant of the fine arts and humanities would soon come to see himself as a part of this knowledgeable group, even though suffering an awed, prosaic bemusement with all three. Though, when mesmerized and existing in a happy state, it may be difficult to know the cause or attraction and like a sideline, parade observer or a sports event attendee, mesmerized into feeling and seeing his taking an active part on the playing field or moving on as part of the parade, rather than merely there to help create an adoring crowd. Whereas he may have dazzled or manipulated, with the appearance of a calm certainty and by native cunning, a few of his insular or parochial friends, there was never enough depth or resources to extend this sham or these affectations beyond a few, within his small, home shire. Though, for those living by illusions and fantasies, this must be quite fulfilling.

There was, however, a small group of writers in Greenville, around the early and mid part of the last century, who were incredible word craftsmen and truly talented. Though never mesmerized by this crowd, its regalia or consumption, they did produce some immortal letters to ring with any of the past, a voice to help civilize us all.

Nevertheless, the planters' real assets and survival were bundled with their friendliness and hospitality, their love of revelry and laughter, of storytelling and sporting, their sustaining ability to tolerate endless boredom and persistent hard work, along with a "sizable portion of mother wit and gumption." They had a certain pride and honor, proud of their families and proud of sustaining themselves by their wits and they needed to affix their name to a paper, only to protect their heirs. A man's word was good, a handshake would seal it. He had a deep and profound love for his family and of his land. His compassion, single minded and unwavering. The love for his family and longing for an heir, however, was oftentimes misguided to the point of grooming a failure for a successor. His family was always first and foremost, the land came next, and he felt nothing but contempt and scorn for the low, miserable wretch who reversed this order. Confronted by illimitable odds, he tenaciously mustered the courage to try again, to persevere and endure, to face any man who would defile his character.

Above all, there was Papa, a lofty exaltation of Papa and what Papa had done and what Papa embodied and what he encompassed and had accomplished. The planter's greatest and lasting ambition, his constant striving, always kept locked within himself, was to best this and his constant hope that Papa would be there to see him do it and congratulate him for it. It is difficult to reckon the grief and despair this idea and striving must have caused.

W. J. Cash, in "The Mind of the South," summed it up well when he stated. "These men took from aristocracy, as much as and no more than, could be made to fit with their own homespun qualities; and so what they took they made solidly their own, without any sense of inadequacy to haunt them into gaucherie. The result was a kindly courtesy, a level eyed pride, an easy quietness of manner, a barely perceptible flourish, of bearing, which for all its obvious angularity and fundamental plainness, was one of the finest things the Old South produced."

They all, liked to think and dream they embodied all of this. It was only the occasional few who ever succeeded. Though more would strive toward it. There was, however, occasionally that uncommon man who seemed to be born with the correct attributes or mettle for leadership and success and now and then a big farmer would achieve this status by skill and effort. But, most filled out only a partial list. The success, though, was in the trying and the battle. But, there were some who never tried, as the Delta had its share of reprobates, habitual drunkards, deadbeats, cotton thieves, congenital liars, bootleggers, and other vile creatures.

Wealth was still held, as it always had been, by the financiers, the people dealing in money up east, some of the oil people, manufacturers, railroad and shipping magnates, and a few huge merchants. This Delta was like old man Joe Kennedy told Roosevelt, "There ain't a million dollars between Memphis and Vicksburg."

But, it was the dawn of the twenties and they would soon begin to roar, to utter a full, loud, prolonged sound, confused and directionless. The Delta would do some of that too, with some stomping added.

Wall Street bankers had all the paper money they wanted now, pushed at them from the newly organized federal reserve, only seven years old, and they would pump it out in torrents, waiting nine more roaring years, before they would again be seized by fear; ageless and blinding fear, immobilizing and groundless, then suddenly cut it all off and call it all back. But, for now fear would be gone for awhile and with a full stomach and good prospects for a hearty breakfast, they would only think about it on Sunday mornings, then only for a short while.

The Kate Adams was on the river, roads were being graveled and cars were moving on them, not in great numbers yet but they were there. Long freight and passenger trains were stopping at every town or hamlet along the rails. You could be in Memphis in four hours. The Peabody would open in 1924 and there was good whiskey in Rosedale.

Credit, Satan's partially reformed second cousin, the one that creates most millionaires and paupers, poverty and prosperity, was soon let loose on the land. Automobiles, radios and movies were being made and they had to be bought and seen. Every town had a high fenced, roofless picture show, an Air Dome, packed full every rainless night. Cars soon became plentiful, so plentiful dealers would sell them out of a cotton house if his showrooms were full. Radios were shipped in by the carload, from Orgill Brothers and Stratton Warren, in Memphis, filling show windows and counters of stores, merchants asking no payment until fall. Every farmer and tenant good for nineteen dollars worth of credit could have one, including a battery and a hundred foot aerial wire. Placed on a front porch in late afternoon during the summer months and after sensitive adjustment and delicately synchronizing four dials, they would draw a crowd at night, listening to music played in Nashville. The crowd would be there until the biting, winged pests of evening finally forced them to leave. The fortunate few to a bed surrounded by a mosquito bar, but without screens or other barriers covering the open windows, and doors, most to suffer the insects all night.

Pig finally began to see clearly what he had surmised all along. He realized he would never be a big cotton farmer and the boom and burst of 1919 had shown that the biggest of them could be wiped out and back in the cotton field in just one year. He knew that hoeing cotton would never buy all he needed. As a young teenager, he began buying a calf or several pigs and selling them after they had grown. Each year the numbers he bought increased and he soon realized that he made some money doing this, much easier than the field. But he saw, too, how he could easily talk somebody into paying more than the animal was worth. He improved this skill and pushed it hard, even out trading older men who had practiced this art for years. Soon he was buying grown animals and selling them the next day or same day, sometimes doubling his money in less than twenty-four hours. He would buy a hog or calf from one tenant, and with its sale to another one, resulting in a high profit, making the seller wait until it was sold for his payment. He bought hogs for two or three dollars and sold them for five or six. While he was still a teenager, he developed into a huckster and the ultimate salesman, selling something for beyond its value, which he never paid, the buyer being appreciative and grateful for the privilege of this special favor and courtesy. He could sell anything, a coop of chickens, a sack full of guineas. He bought and sold turkeys and geese, kept a yard full of ducks.

He caught a stray mule once, fed him well, keeping him hidden in the barn. When, after several weeks nobody claimed him, he decided to sell him. He spread the word around the area that he had a fine mule for sale and several small farmers came by to look at the animal. After several more weeks the story circulated in an even wider circle and, with no claimants, he felt the mule was surely his. Information soon reached all the way to Clarksdale, about the boy down at Lewis' Swamp who had a fine mule to sell. Before long, two farmers came down to look at Pig's mule. They met the old man who took them around to the barn and Pig ran there to greet them. "This here's Mr. Lodge Lowery," the old man said. "He wants to look at yore mule." Pig ran up to the farmer and grabbed his hand, a wide grin covering his entire face. "And this here's Mr. Jeremiah Provine," he continued, as Pig grabbed his hand just as hard.

"Good to make ya'lls 'quaintance, Mr. Lodge. I sho got a fine mule in here. You gonna want to see 'im." Pig was barefooted, had on a pair of overalls held up by one gallus, a torn shirt open down to the top of the bib because of no button, and he looked like a little twelve or fourteen year old, fat boy standing there. He and Lodge walked into the barn.

The ground was covered with dried manure and trampled hay, but his bare feet easily moved on it, and he stood as easily as if he had on shoes. After they were in the barn, he turned and looked up at the farmer, as his entire face again turned into a wide grin. "Well, there he is, standin' yonder. Ain't he pretty?" Lodge looked back at the little boy and grinned as he walked on over toward the mule. He and Pig stood looking at the animal and the old man and Jeremiah waited outside. When Jeremiah saw the owner of the mule was only a small boy, he felt sorry for him and told the old man, "You better go in there and talk for that boy. My buddy's an old mule trader and he'll beat 'im outta that mule." The old man looked at him and grinned. "We'll just watch 'im for awhile and see."

Pig had brushed the mule well, his coat shining and smooth, glistening in the light of the barn. He had sheared his mane close, to a fine pointed ridge. His hooves were trimmed even and none had any splits. Pig walked up to the mule, held out his hand toward him, still with his broad grin like he was trying to calm him or ingratiate himself with the animal. But it wasn't the animal whose favor he wanted. He slowly put his hands on the mule's nose and gradually rubbed them down to open his mouth. Pig had practiced this many times with the animal and he stood there quietly while Pig showed his teeth. "Looka here at his teeth. This mule is young. Ain't no mor'n five or six years old." He rubbed his shoulders and neck as he said, "Ain't a collar sore been on 'im nowhere."

After rubbing his neck and shoulders, he slowly moved his hand back on the mule's lower ribs and side and gently rubbing the creature said again, "He's been well took care of. Ain't no trace chains ever rubbed 'im too much, ain't galled nowhere." Lodge examined him for awhile, looking closely at both sides and both ends. Then Pig led him around by a short rope on his bridle to show how the mule could walk. After a brief time, Lodge stepped back and said, "How much do you want for him?" Pig was standing there still rubbing the beast's nose and did not answer him or look up. He acted as if he never heard him, as if he were merely showing the mule in a circus or mule show. After a short while Lodge asked again, "Well, what do you want for him, son?" Pig pretended not to hear him still, for a short while and then, holding the short rope, he stepped back and still looking at the mule, squarely in his face, he slowly mumbled, "You know, I jus may not sell this mule." "I thought you wuz wantin' to sell 'im?" Lodge almost shouted. Pig cocked his head to one side while still looking at the mule's face and with his toothy grin he said, "Well, I did want to sell 'im, but he looks mighty good, don't he? Why, this young mule could plow another fifteen or sixteen years." Lodge was walking around him now, looking at the mule real close. "Yeah, he looks all right, he could prob'ly plow a pretty good while." Pig kept looking at the mule's drawn out, coffin-shaped face, the ears 10 inches long, both pointed together, straight upward, while he rubbed him across his soft, downy nose. Lodge, still slowly circling the mule, asked him again what he wanted for him. This time, leaving no doubt, even for a deaf man, to know what he said, "I'm still not sure I wanna sell 'im," Pig answered after awhile, still grinning and rubbing the mule's nose. "But if'n I did wanna sell 'im," he said slowly, "whadda you think he might be worth?" Lodge looked up at him and walked a little faster around the mule, as if to get a better look, in order to make a bid on him. After awhile of circling and looking, he said to Pig, "Is that mule broke to a plow?" "We been plowin' 'im several years," Pig answered. "He plows good." "Has he ever pulled a cultivator with another mule?" "Yeah," Pig answered, "we plow 'im with another mule alla time. Pulls a cultivator good." Pig kept his wide grin. Lodge kept circling and finally said, "Why that mule may be worth a hundred dollars." Pig, still grinning and rubbing the mule, said, "A hundred dollars?" he thought.

He leisurely put his hand on the bridle between the mule's long ears as he sluggishly continued rubbing his face. He acted as he would take the bridle off and turn the mule back into pasture, but Lodge quickly stopped him. "Well, son, he might be worth a little more than that. Let me look at him again." He rounded the mule again several times and Pig showed him the animal's teeth. "Them teeth's in good shape," he said as Lodge bent down and looked in the mule's mouth. "Yeah, they look all right," he said. "They look good, don't they?" Pig quickly added. "Yeah, they'll do," he said. Lodge kept looking and after awhile he offered, "Well, since I done looked at him pretty good, I'd say he might go for a hundred and fifty." With that, Pig began to pull on the bridle, as Lodge anxiously watched him. "Or in a tight," he added, "he might jus go for two hundred dollars." Pig kept his hand on the bridle, between the mule's ears, but slackened it slightly, his arm in a position where the farmer could easily see it. "Well, I believe this here mule is worth more than that," Pig quipped. "He could plow a long time. You know, the more I think about it, the better this mule looks," he added. "I could make a lotta cotton with this mule and they say cotton's likely to go up again." Lodge walked up to the mule and rubbed him across his back and down his flank and hip. Pig had his dark brown coat brushed to a fine glisten as Lodge easily rubbed him and stood on his toes to look over his shoulders.

The old man and Jeremiah were watching as this jousting went back and forth and the old man looked at him and, raising his eyebrows, nodded his head. Jeremiah merely shook his head and both continued their vigil.

Pig kept rubbing the mule's face and moved his fat hand softly and gently across the flaccid, supple velvet of his nose. "You know, mister," he mentioned, "I got this mule when he wud'n nothin' but a colt and fed 'im, took care of 'im, and raised 'im. I broke 'im in dat field over yonder four or five winters ago when it wad'n nothin' but knee deep mud. Broke him to a saddle too. Why, this mule's a good saddle mule. You can ride 'im anywhere you wanna go. You could even ride this mule to church. He'll stand, too. Stand wherever you put 'im and he ain't bad 'bout brayin' either. He'll stand in a churchyard all day Sunday with a saddle on 'im and won't say nothin'."

Pig had Lodge's attention again. He stopped walking and, turning his head toward Pig who continued holding the bridle while slowly rubbing, asked, "You mean this mule is broke to a saddle?" "Got a gait smooth as most good saddle horses," Pig answered. Lodge squinted his eye and stared at Pig a little more intently. "I been needin' a good saddle horse, could ride him to the store rather than goin' in that wagon. Has he got a pretty good gait?" he asked. "Like I say, he's got a good gait, smooth as some saddle horses. I taught 'im myself, ridin' 'im alla time. He can cover the ground, too." Lodge's circling slowly continued as he rounded the mule and had Pig show his teeth again. Then, standing next to Pig and looking straight at him, he questioned again, "Well, what will ya take for him?"

Pig turned away, back toward the mule and while still holding the bridle between his ears, his broad grin still beaming, he gently patted the mule's face as he said, "You know, I'm jus not sure yet 'bout sellin' this mule. Why, mister, he's got a smooth gait, better'n most good saddle horses, smooth as settin' in a rockin' chair." Pig continued grinning, but he thought he had pushed about as hard as he could, before he commented, "With all that, a good saddle mule, a good plow mule, whadda you think he might be worth?" Lodge circled once more, slowly shaking his head. "Well, son, I'll tell ya," he finally answered, "since he can do all that, a good saddle mule, a good plow mule too, broke to a walking or riding cultivator, he might be worth three hundred dollars." Pig's eyes danced a little, his grin even broadened when he heard this.

Three hundred dollars, he thought. Why, you could buy a team of good, paired mules for four or five hundred. Pig held onto the bridle between his ears and continued rubbing as he finally answered, "Well, we might talk some on that, but I sho do hate to get shut of this here mule since I raised 'im and had 'im so long." Lodge and Pig talked on awhile longer, Pig rubbing and patting the mule's face and nose, and Lodge continuing to circle the mule, sometimes stopping to talk or ask another question.

The joust was over. Pig took his hand off of the bridle, when Lodge gave him three hundred and fifty dollars and Peg handed him the lead rope. Pig stepped back, his grin as wide as ever, and Lodge led his high priced mule toward the door.

Of the two standing at the door keeping watch, the old man walked away, with a rare grin on his face, Jeremiah stood there, just shaking his head as he murmured, "I never seed nothin' like that."

Pig was in business now. He had a little money. He bought a second hand Model T Ford truck. It was in good shape, nearly new, but the farmer who owned it was in a bind and Pig took it off of his hands for a hundred and fifty dollars. It would carry over a thousand pounds and pull a two wheel trailer that he made carrying the same amount. With the tall sides he built for both of them, it would carry three or four half grown cows or steers. Pig left the cotton field, he was finished with cotton forever. He could sell anything. He sold clothes, furniture, cooking utensils. He had a rolling store. Even sold a tenant a pair of false teeth and filed them and sanded them until they fit.

Always grinning, with a quiet story and now chomping on a cigar. By the early thirties he had left the swamp settlement and moved to Hushpuckena to operate a service station on a gravel road just as it crossed a railroad track and turned south to run parallel to it. The gravel road was the original US Highway 61 and four or five Greyhound buses passed each day, his station serving as the bus stop. He had a helper, a hired man, to run his station, most of the time and he stayed in his truck, on the road, buying and selling whatever he could. He was married now, had several small children.

During the early to mid thirties a market rapidly developed for scrap iron and any other metal. Most of it shipped to Japan, nobody ever questioning what they wanted with all that scrap. If they would pay for it, we would sell it to them. The price kept going up each year and the country was full of it. None had ever been worth anything before. Pig was in the scrap iron business early and would easily double or triple his money on each trade. Nobody knew what it was worth and he could buy it for about the price of hauling it off. He always said that he never made but four percent, bought it for one dollar and sold it for four. Pig had heard that all the banks made six to eight percent and he always thought he was paying too much for the iron.

Pig bought so much iron he soon had a new name. Mr. Pig Iron. He was buying and shipping scrap iron by the car load, from a railroad sidetrack, in Hushpuckena. Truck and wagon loads were coming in from miles away. Old iron that had been lying around farm headquarters and junk piles for years soon became a valuable commodity. He continued to run his truck, too, on regular routes all over the country, buying iron and carrying the message of its value. He also bought aluminum, copper, and lead, old car batteries. With these being in much smaller quantities, he took this always to a Clarksdale dealer. Pig bought old plow tools, motors, gin stands. All the gins at one time had steam engines, replaced now by Fairbanks Morse diesels.

There was always a giant discarded steam boiler close by each one, lying there turning to rust. Pig bought them for about the price of hauling them away. With his acetylene torch he would soon have a giant ten ton boiler in small pieces and he could carry it bit by bit to the railroad. Borrowing trucks from some of his friends for nothing, he would have a line going back and forth to the railroad like a line of ants carrying off a small pile of sugar that would suddenly disappear. Pig used his torch to sell anything. He would cut up old car bodies and ship them out. Railroad hardware was a different commodity, you could not give him any of that. To have a railroad inspector looking down at him would be akin to seeing one of J. Edgar Hoover's boys approaching. He did not want that. He always kept one step ahead of it. He bought so much junk he was cleaning up the entire county. Pig was somebody now, Mr. Pig Iron, the big man in scrap iron, a true heavyweight, and the word literally fit him.

He did not relinquish his cattle and hog buying. He just got better at it. He had a 1932 Chevrolet truck and with it, he had bought or sold, traded or swapped something with every tenant in the county. They all knew him and each thought they had thrashed him in a deal, when actually they had been well cleaned by Mr. Pig Iron. They had usually submitted to a thorough cleaning, losing both their britches and their shoes in the process and when Pig got through with them they seemed thankful and grateful that they had been allowed to do business with Mr. Pig Iron, but bragging that they had beat him and boastful that they were left with something.

Pig Iron had a globular, grungy face, loose and slack, but he could tighten it when needed, except for the pendulous jowls that hung down on his shirt collar, when he wore one, his raven black ebony eyes set high on his forehead, tight together, piercing and roving, but with the light of a ready grin, when needed. They could turn from thoughtful seriousness to wild howling laughter in an instant, when it served his purpose, negotiating the last dime on a wagon load of iron or a man's good milk cow. In a barn lot with twenty or thirty hogs or cattle he could pick out the one animal worth a dollar more than any other and paying half price for it, the tenant would think he had gotten a clear satisfaction and beat him when he would chomp down on his short stubby cigar, furrow his narrow thick brow, and wonder aloud how he would shoe and clothe his family after paying so much for this poor critter. Loud blandished, blazonry, with quiet, ingratiating deceit was the center of his business, his livelihood, his work. He was an expert at it, survived on it, loved it. Those "poor simpletons" were easy prey for his guile and chicanery. But, the tenant always believed, "I done beat him agin, I'll beat Mr. Pig Iron next time, too." It was easy for Pig Iron, he had practiced his art thoroughly and, "I done took 'em all, all of 'em," he boastfully repeated. The tenant did not have a chance.

There were several, though, that knew Mr. Pig Iron, had a sound understanding of him. Gordon Monach, a tenant, known by all his friends as "Mr. Gold Money," was well acquainted with him and asked a friend, who had a young hog nearly grown, that Mr. Pig Iron was trying to buy, "What did he offer you for him?" "Well, Mr. Pig Iron said that he waddin nothin' but a shoat and even big shoats waddin worth nothin' much, 'bout a dollar and a quarter." "Why, dat's nearly a grown hog you got. You know I done seed him," Gold Money answered. They were walking down a dirt road, half a mile from any other human, as Gold Money lowered his voice, to almost a whisper, and continued, "Why, dat Pig Iron ain't nuthin but a liar, a vitrified liar. Dat's the worse kinda liar day is." Gold Money continued, "A vitrified liar will tell a compound lie." "What kinda lie is dat?" his friend asked. "A compound lie," he answered, "dat's tellin' one lie to cover up another one. Dat's a vitrified lie and it'll send a man straight to Hades. Dat's fo miles the other side- a Hell. Dat white man orta be in the pen-tenchary for all dat lyin'." Nonetheless, Pig later bought the five dollar hog for a dollar and a half.

The next week Gold Money was working in his field hoeing cotton not far from his house when Pig Iron came by on his route. His truck was only half loaded with scrap iron and junk as he roared along just ahead of a cloud of dust. Never wanting to miss a chance to find something and get it, he turned his truck, off the dusty, deep rutted, section line road onto the narrow wagon path, between rows of waist high July cotton, leading to Gold Money's house.

An aged and weathered, paling fence surrounded it, the palings parallel and lined straight as a stilled pendulum in a tall old clock. Standing upright, close together and erect, perpendicular to the flat alluvial earth across which they ran. The corners square and sharp as if laid out with pride and self assurance, the plumbed, palings surrounding almost an acre. They were of red cedar rived from three foot thick logs, but now faded and stained, weather worn and hardened, long since having lost all but a trace of the sweet, aromatic, effusive scent still locked forever inside the ancient wood. Void of any worm damage or decay seen in all other old Delta woods except that of the cypress, whose primeval foliage appears, then is later lost in the dark, watery, sodden swamps and will survive as sawed timber, dark and solid, three hundred years even in the same surroundings.

A canopy of chinaberry trees surrounded the house, their thick tiny leaves dark and night, green, blocking any summer ray to the wood shingled two sided roof and pottery hard, broom swept yard below. Sagging, soap scrubbed steps and a vine covered porch approached the door to the central room of the house. Clean, though cluttered, and with the rank acrid odor of burnt wood and ashes mixed with that of long unwashed human flesh. The balance of the house, only two small crypt like cubicles on opposite sides and a low ceilinged dark space, at the rear, a chimneyed kitchen, where below its door two old bricks stepped to the hard, broom swept earth outside.

Opposite the one windowed wall of the central room, fixed high by a single nail, hung the only picture in the house. A picture of the Mississippi Congressional Delegation of 1868. Positioned head high, demanding anyone entering the room see it, look and gaze upon it and wonder what or who it was, to come closer to the dark gold painted, dusty, old, framed picture covered with a bulging domed glass to read under it, if he could read, and see the five men there, dressed in Prince Albert broadcloth who were the entire Mississippi Congressional Delegation of that year. The state of Mississippi's elected representatives to the National Congress in Washington. All black, with full gray beards, the five gazed down upon the room in their Victorian vestments, with pendulous watch chains across their vests and Abe Lincoln bow ties. A permanent sentinel, with self assured dignity, a constant reminder and fervent hope, positioned to be seen by any entrant to the room.

The house was surrounded by the spreading flat, unwrinkled, 20 acre field of solid, dark green, soon to the laid by, July cotton. From a distance, the tree canopied house with its tight, weathered, paling fence emerged from the level cotton field like an oasis on a straight desert horizon.

"How 'bout gettin' a drink o' water from your pump?" Pig Iron asked. "Yessir, hep yerself. Go ahead," Gold Money answered. He bent over, primed the hand pump, and pumped awhile until the water ran cold. As he bent over to take a drink, he saw a dull, silver pot, a big teakettle, sitting there on the wet, muddy ground, beside the pump runoff. It sat circular and wide, mud splattered, tall on the wet ground. Its lower portion in the mud, rounding upward, high and closing inward toward the mouth like, much smaller circular orifice at its peak. Vertical walls inside the circular, mouth like orifice, curved straight down, algae green, to the dark, reflective, still surface of the water inside. He saw the small circle deep within the kettle, dark but reflecting segments of blue, July sky and clear, green chinaberry limbs. A cylindrical spout came big, out of the mud, arching upward in an S-shape to become smaller and open as it curved horizontal again. A steel handle causing the only iron rust on the kettle lay stagnant and coiled against a dull, silver gray, expanded wall of aluminum, rust stained by the iron and tarnished below it. He stared at it awhile, rolled his beady eyes off toward the tree line beyond the field, blinked two or three times to be sure they were clear, and strained his eyes back at the kettle again, hoping Gold Money would not notice his excitement.

"I'll be damned," he thought, "looka here. A five gallon 'luminum kettle with sides three inches thick. So thick, I bet it won't hold a quart of water. Why, that's solid 'luminum. It'll hafta weigh ten pounds and that stuff is worth two bits a pound. That's two dollars and a half. Momma had one jus like it, holds six teacups of water hot all day, 'luminum'll hold heat." He was bent over, still drinking, while he eyed the huge kettle Gold Money used to water his chickens. He then stood up, faced the field and called to him. "Gold Money, come over here a minute. I wanna talk to you." As he stood up, he kicked at the kettle, picked it up, mud clinging to its leaden, aluminum flanks. Sure enough, it was massive. "This thang is heavy," he thought, "walls thick as a skillet cooked hoecake. It might weigh twelve maybe fourteen pounds." He knew he had found something valuable, maybe a week's wage. Aluminum had been going up for the past year and a half. It had gone from ten to over twenty-five cents a pound since he had been selling it.

"Mr. Pig Iron, how you been doin'?" Gold Money said as he touched the brim of his sweat stained straw hat. "Doin' good. How 'bout you?" Gold Money stared at him, watching hard. Pig Iron's evasive eyes focused on the teakettle.

"Well, Mr. Pig Iron, what did ya want? I gotta work." "Gold Money, I wuz jus lookin' at this little ol' teakettle you got here watering all these chickens. Don't look like it holds much water, 'bout empty." "Yessir, it is." Gold Money never looked at the kettle.

"I wuz jus thinkin' as I got me a drank. I ain't got but a few chickens and it'd sho' make a good waterin' trough for mine. It'd sho be a favor if you'd let me buy it off of ya." "Aw, you don't want dat waterin' pot, Mr. Pig Iron, it ain't worth nothin'." "I know it ain't worth nothin'," Pig Iron said, "but I could sho use it and I'll pay ya for it. Tell ya what. Since it ain't no good, aint' worth nothin' and I could use it, I'll give ya fifteen cents for it, just like it is, to show you where my heart is, to hep ya out that much."

Gold Money now began to eye Pig Iron and to watch him carefully. Pig Iron slowly walked around the thick aluminum teakettle, glancing down at it like a hawk watching a rabbit. Then he would back away and spit on the ground, moving around it again. Gold Money was watching him with side glances. Pig Iron's eyes would focus on the kettle, his narrow, thick brow furrowed, like rows in a plowed field. Then he chomped on his burnt out cigar and took a few side steps away from it, then partially circling it again. He spit once more, hitting a chicken eight feet away. Pig Iron was studying the kettle like a man studying a thoroughbred race horse before he buys it. He circled it again, hands in his pockets, spreading his britches wide, like a cavalry officer's, in full riding attire. Walking out a few paces toward the cotton field, he said to Gold Money, "Sho is some pretty cotton ya got there. Ya orta make a bale and a half."

Gold Money didn't answer, did not even look at him. But as Pig Iron turned back toward the kettle he again glanced toward him and saw those beady eyes jumping. A narrow forehead, furrowed deep as he gaped and stared straight at the kettle.

"Tell ya what I'll do, Gold Money. I'll give you twenty cents for that lil ol' wo' out tea kettle." He said nothing else about how he wanted to help him, how good his heart was, just looked at the kettle and then at Gold Money. "Well, Mr. Pig Iron, I know dat pot ain't worth much but I done had it so long and I made out with it. 'Sides, dat thang's too big and heavy for you to fool with." When Gold Money said that, Pig Iron had to turn and stare again at it. "That thang is heavy," he thought, "look how it sinks down in that mud." Once more he walked over and picked it up, leaned it over as if he was trying to see how much water it would hold, as Gold Money watched him. "This kettle is heavy, maybe more than I thought. It could weigh fourteen pounds," he mumbled to himself. "This lil ol' tea kettle ain't so heavy," Pig Iron said, "but I sho could use it to water my chickens and it ain't big enough for yours. I'll bet you fillin' it up all day. Whadda you say? Twenty cents and I'll take it outa your way, hep clean up your yard." Gold Money stared down at him. Pig Iron's beady eyes grinning, bracing himself with a hand on one knee, the kettle held in the other, as he stood in the mud. "Well, I don't know 'bout it, Mr. Pig Iron," Gold Money answered. "I jus don't know. Dat pot bein' made outa solid 'luminum and all and since I done had it so long." He stared at the pot and seemed to think about it awhile, then turned and walked slowly toward his back fence, the paling higher than the front of the yard, but he could easily see over it, his cotton rows converging in the distance toward the creek.

A subtle July breeze moved through the chinaberry branches vibrating the tiny leaves into a high pitched whistling sound, like wind through tall juniper bushes, their fall foliage stiff and rigid, almost wooden, the tiny projections vibrating like reeds in a woodwind. He felt the breeze on his narrow face, dry and cool against his moist, light ginger skin. He stood there tall and thin, eyes fixed to the outlying horizon, as if gazing at far off herds or even a distant mirage, as his North African, horsemen bloodline, for two hundred generations, had done. He had owned that pot a long time, he thought, found it in a trash pile over by Hushpuckena Creek bridge. But it was old then, he could always get something else to water his chickens. Besides, a little money would come in handy. That pot may go to leaking, too, he thought, it stays muddy around it all the time now, didn't used to. If it went to leaking it wouldn't be no good for watering the chickens. Have to fill it up too much.

Pig Iron hadn't moved, not even straightened up, stood there, both feet set firm in the mud, bent over holding the kettle. Gold Money turned back toward him, his face expressionless, board like. His jaw did not move up or down as he spoke, just opened. "I think the man dat gets this here pot will have to pay twenty-five cents. Yessir, that's one quarter of a dollar."

Pig Iron knew, he had him. Gold Money thought he had set the price for the pot, but that had been done when they first started talking. Pig Iron dropped the kettle back in the mud, stood up and said, "Why, Gold Money, you ort not do me like that. I cain't pay no quarter for a lil 'ol tea kettle like this. Ain't worth it." He looked down at the kettle, shook his head, "Naw sir, ain't worth it." He stood there a short while, shook his head again, "Naw sir, cain't do it," then slowly turned back toward his truck. Halfway there, he turned once again. "Twenty cents, Gold Money, twenty, hard earned cents." "Naw sir, cain't do it, cain't take no less than a quarter, Mr. Pig Iron." When he got to his truck he reached for the door handle, but turned before he touched it. He took a longer time walking the short distance back.

Neither said anything until he was within two feet of the kettle. "You done beat me, Gold Money," and he shook his head as he slowly said his name, "You done beat me bad. Here's yer quarter. I'll hep ya that much." He picked up the pot, placed it gently in his truck and drove off. Driving home he thought, "That tea kettle's heavy, maybe it'll weigh fifteen pounds. If aluminum has gone up to thirty cents, that would be uh, let me see, a good day's work. A man don't make that much money plowing a mule all week and all day Saturday."

Pig Iron had done it again, cut a deal, made a trade, greased the scaly, rough surfaces, the interface of human contact and both sides better for it. Two men once more found a necessary, prized and valued, then later coveted, commodity. The one needing utility, service, value, long ago. The other a self assured pilferer, devious in the ways and usage of bargaining and stealth, just now. With possession changed, not by brute force or violent, primitive barbarity, but rather by gentlemanly, cultivated haggling and dickering and cunning, they parted. Each happy in the knowledge he had bettered his rival and for now content with his reward. There had been a tournament, a joust, a hard, unyielding and widely maneuvered skirmish with no visible blood on the field, a civilized contest, evolved to permit battle, while saving skin and limb and life, with pride and self esteem intact, enhanced and elevated.

An endeavor organized and old when heavy, laden Phoenician boats pushed out of the walled ports of Sidon and Tyre, plowed the ancient Mediterranean, unloaded and reloaded at Cypress, Rhodes and Crete, then on to Carthage, Corsica and Spain. The magnet of exchange and trade then pulled these deep vessels through the strait, on to the uncharted cold of the North Atlantic. An alphabet bartered for a fur. An eternity of knowledge for an evaporated instant, leaving both groups jubilant, in their triumph. The seed took hold, germinated, then put forth and endured to struggle on.

Pig Iron was up early Saturday morning, had to drive twenty miles, due north, on new Highway 61, to Bloom Brothers junkyard at Clarksdale. He loaded the truck the day before. It was crammed full, stuffed high with copper telegraph wire, and chunks of lead he melted down from old car batteries and a few big pieces of iron he brought along just to keep check on the price. Up close to the cab of the truck with nothing on top of it, on the outside corner, away from the passing traffic sat his prize, his shiny aluminum teakettle. He spent several hours the night before rubbing it with a croker sack to put a coarse shine on it, then polishing it more, with a close weave cloth, bringing out the glistening brilliance of rubbed aluminum. He knew he would get a week's wages, maybe more, for the fifteen pound kettle.

His son, Sonny Boy, a 10-year-old, 40 pounder, was up and dressed, new overalls and a new shirt, but barefooted, when Pig made his coffee that morning. The boy's mother had bought the new clothes at Yaffe and Rosen's, the only singularly, dry goods store in Hushpuckena, but she could have bought them at any of the three other general merchandise stores there. However, Pig already owed them too much, consequently she went to the only store where he owed nothing, Yaffee and Rosen's, as they did not sell on credit. A half hour or so after daybreak the 1932 Chevrolet truck was full of gas, cranked, and moved off toward Clarksdale. They had no flats to delay them and that truck hummed smooth, all the way, like a close set sewing machine.

Pig Iron couldn't wait to walk through the junkyard carrying his wash tub sized kettle. He knew the yard would be full on Saturday morning. He decided he would just back his truck into the yard and let the hands there unload it while he walked around carrying the tea kettle. "I'm gonna let em all see this kettle," he told Sonny Boy.

There was row upon row of iron stacked in the yard and he planned to casually walk down most of them, putting his kettle on grand exhibition. After he had done that, had them all looking, he might just walk on up front in the office, sit down and talk to one of the Bloom boys awhile, about the price of iron and copper. He would set the big shiny kettle down, sort of behind him, so they would all have to look around to see it. They probably had not seen that much aluminum all year, he thought. Then after awhile, when he had gathered a crowd, he would take the kettle on back, put it on the scales, stand back and watch them weigh it.

Not having to stop once, in less than an hour, they were in Clarksdale. As they came up, from beneath the railroad overpass they saw it. The Bloom Brothers building. It stood there just south of the highway, tall and dominant, almost sovereign, as it had done for the past forty years. Every junk dealer and scrap iron collector in North Mississippi knew where it was and within its chambers, upon its tables, had traded junk for money. It just seemed to materialize there, to burst upon them, as they suddenly came from beneath the overpass.

The appearance of the building was lofty and striking, that Saturday morning, with its buff yellow brick facade, outlined and forcefully detailed by the radiance of the mid morning, July sun. Tall plate glass windows and entrance were placed between two broad stainless steel columns. The steel surfaces etched, as if to appear like stone and massive enough to have been placed by Solomon himself. The columns extended forty feet into the air, to a wide crown, in whose center a fifty foot indentation was impressed, with the words BLOOM BROTHERS spread across it, in massive embossed lettering, as if sculptured or engraved in bold relief. From each side of the front of the building, a ten foot high, steel paneled, mesh fence extended outward seventy-five feet, then turned exactly ninety degrees in two other plumbed lines, which stretched rearward, seemingly projecting the building closer to the highway and even taller, completely enclosing the junk yard and totally cloaking it, behind this towering shield. It could easily have been in Memphis, along South Main, on the bluffs, with a name like

Goldsmith's or Lowenstein's or Levy's. Time had not effaced hope but only overshadowed it with a longing for means and status and recognition.

The only entrance for traders being a gated opening at the rear of the fence completely obscuring the nature of the enterprise which may have been anything, though from its veneer and perspective, it had to be something uplifting and grand. "So it was," the Bloom boys said, "making money."

Pig Iron drove his truck through the entrance at the back gate, to await his turn being unloaded, turned off the motor, got his polished kettle and with Sonny Boy behind him, started his trek through the yard. Proceeding exactly as he had planned, he had a fair sized crowd, a dozen or more, even one of the Bloom brothers was with him, when he set the bright kettle on the scales and stepped back to admire his prize, hands in his pocket, as he strutted around spreading his britches wide, in jodhpur fashion.

One of the workmen in the crowd following him never broke stride, when Pig Iron placed the kettle on the scales, but continued forward, reached down, picked it up and felt inside. He walked about five paces further, picked up a small hammer, struck the pot hard, one solid blow.

Pig Iron saw it, when it happened. A dull sound, then instantly, a cloud of dust shot up out of the pot like a whirlwind down a July, dirt road. Two or three more blows and the pot was full of broken, brick like, pottery material. The thin aluminum covering had been lined with three inches of stone hard, fired clay. Now, all ballast, it was emptied out and when the dust settled the workman placed the beaten aluminum shell on the scales. It was so light it sounded like an empty, tin can when placed on the iron surface. The crowd left. Pig Iron, Sonny Boy and the workman stood there, but only the Bloom Brothers man read the scale.

Sonny Boy and his daddy waited in the truck for one of the employees to bring their money and receipt. They didn't have to wait long. It was handed to them in a long, white, Bloom Brothers envelope and they headed for home.

They were nearly there when Pig Iron opened it and mumbled to himself as he read, "Seven hundred and sixty-two pounds of scrap iron at forty cents a hundred-three dollars and a nickel. Forty-two pounds of copper at eight cents a pound—three dollars and thirty-six cents. Fourteen pounds of lead at ten cents a pound—a dollar forty. Then; Aluminum: at thirty-two cents a pound, three quarters pound—twenty-four cents."

The cigar stub dropped from his mouth when he cursed and nearly took his eyes off the road, but he managed to keep the truck out of the ditch. "Son, did you see that?" he bellowed. "Did you see what that nigger did to my kettle? And that Jew made 'im do it."

Sonny Boy, gazing out of a window, never heard his voice over the hum of the motor and the rush of air through an open window. "Like I been tryin' to tell ya, boy, you gotta watch them folks, you gotta watch 'em close. They'll beat ya. They'll beat ya ever chance they git."